TEXTS FOR
COMMON PRAYER

Containing Forms for
DAILY MORNING PRAYER
DAILY EVENING PRAYER
and THE HOLY COMMUNION as
Approved by the College of Bishops
for Use within the Province
Together with
THE ORDINAL
of the

ANGLICAN CHURCH
IN NORTH AMERICA

A.D. 2013

Published by Anglican House Publishers, Inc.
Newport Beach, California.
You may contact us at http://www.ahpub.org
Text set in Garamond typeface. Printed in Korea.

Anglican House
Publishers

ISBN 978-0-9860441-0-6

Table of Contents

With the exception of The Ordinal, which has been authorized and adopted, and is The Ordinal of the Province, the other materials offered in Texts for Common Prayer *are "working texts" approved for use by the College of Bishops. These working texts are not yet finalized, awaiting response from the experience of their wide use in the Church. With that in mind, these rites are commended as appropriate forms for worship in the present season. The Archbishop's instruction to the Liturgy and Common Worship Task Force was the production of rites that were "so faithful and attractive that the Church would want to use them." The hope in making* Texts for Common Prayer *available now is to give evidence that the assignment is well under way, and to invite the whole Body of Christ into the process of receiving and perfecting. Comments may be sent to the Task Force,* liturgytaskforce@anglicanchurch.net.

Daily Morning Prayer

Approved for Provincial Use

The Anglican Church in North America

Petertide, A.D. 2013

The Officiant may begin Morning Prayer by reading an opening sentence of Scripture found on pages 17-19 or another appropriate Scripture. The Confession of Sin may be said, or the Office may continue with "O Lord, open our lips."

Confession of Sin

The Officiant says to the People

Dearly beloved, the Scriptures teach us to acknowledge our many sins and offenses, not concealing them from our heavenly Father, but confessing them with humble and obedient hearts that we may obtain forgiveness by his infinite goodness and mercy. We ought at all times humbly to acknowledge our sins before Almighty God, but especially when we come together in his presence to give thanks for the great benefits we have received at his hands, to declare his most worthy praise, to hear his holy Word, and to ask, for ourselves and others, those things necessary for our life and our salvation. Therefore, come with me to the throne of heavenly grace.

or this

Let us humbly confess our sins to Almighty God.

Silence is kept. All kneeling the Officiant and People say

Almighty and most merciful Father,
we have erred and strayed from your ways like lost sheep.
we have followed too much the deceits and desires of our
    own hearts.

we have offended against your holy laws.
we have left undone those things which we ought to have done,
and we have done those things which we ought not to have done;
and apart from your grace, there is no health in us.
O Lord, have mercy upon us.
Spare those who confess their faults.
Restore those who are penitent, according to your promises declared
    to all people in Christ Jesus our Lord;
And grant, O most merciful Father, for his sake,
    that we may now live a godly, righteous, and sober life,
    to the glory of your holy Name. Amen.

The Priest alone stands and says

Almighty God, the Father of our Lord Jesus Christ, desires not the death of sinners, but that they may turn from their wickedness and live. He has empowered and commanded his ministers to pronounce to his people, being penitent, the absolution and remission of their sins. He pardons all who truly repent and genuinely believe his holy Gospel. For this reason, we beseech him to grant us true repentance and his Holy Spirit, that our present deeds may please him, the rest of our lives may be pure and holy, and that at the last we may come to his eternal joy; through Jesus Christ our Lord. *Amen.*

or this

The Almighty and merciful Lord grant you absolution and remission of all your sins, true repentance, amendment of life, and the grace and consolation of his Holy Spirit. *Amen.*

A deacon or layperson remains kneeling and prays

Grant your faithful people, merciful Lord, pardon and peace; that we may be cleansed from all our sins, and serve you with a quiet mind; through Jesus Christ our Lord. *Amen.*

The Invitatory

All stand.

Officiant	O Lord, open our lips;
People	And our mouth shall proclaim your praise.
Officiant	O God, make speed to save us;
People	O Lord, make haste to help us.
Officiant	Glory to the Father, and to the Son, and to the Holy Spirit;
People	As it was in the beginning, is now, and ever shall be, world without end. Amen.
Officiant	Praise the Lord.
People	The Lord's name be praised.

Then follows the Venite. Alternatively, the Jubilate may be used.

These seasonal antiphons may be sung or said before and after the Invitatory Psalm.

Advent

Our King and Savior now draws near: O come, let us adore him.

Christmas

Alleluia, to us a child is born: O come, let us adore him. Alleluia.

Epiphany through the Baptism of Christ and the Transfiguration

The Lord has shown forth his glory: O come, let us adore him.

Lent

The Lord is full of compassion and mercy: O come, let us adore him.

Easter until Ascension

Alleluia. The Lord is risen indeed: O come, let us adore him. Alleluia.

Ascension until Pentecost

Alleluia. Christ the Lord has ascended into heaven: O come, let us adore him. Alleluia.

Alleluia. The Spirit of the Lord renews the face of the earth: O come, let us adore him. Alleluia.

Trinity Sunday

Father, Son and Holy Spirit, one God: O come, let us adore him.

On feasts of the Incarnation

The Word was made flesh and dwelt among us: O come, let us adore him.

On All Saints and other major saints' days

The Lord is glorious in his saints: O come, let us adore him.

Venite   *O Come*

Psalm 95:1-7; 8-11

O come, let us sing to the Lord;
Let us make a joyful noise to the rock of our salvation!
Let us come into his presence with thanksgiving;
Let us make a joyful noise to him with songs of praise!
For the Lord is a great God, and a great King above all gods.
In his hand are the depths of the earth;
    the heights of the mountains are his also.
The sea is his, for he made it,
    and his hands formed the dry land.
O come, let us worship and bow down;
    Let us kneel before the Lord, our Maker!
For he is our God, and we are the people of his pasture,
    and the sheep of his hand.
O, that today you would hearken to his voice!

In Lent, and on other penitential occasions, the following verses are added.

Do not harden your hearts, as at Meribah,
    as on the day at Massah in the wilderness,

when your fathers put me to the test
and put me to the proof, though they had seen my work.
For forty years I loathed that generation
and said, "They are a people who go astray in their heart,
and they have not known my ways."
Therefore I swore in my wrath,
"They shall not enter my rest."

or this

Jubilate *Be Joyful*

Psalm 100

Be joyful in the Lord, all you lands;
serve the Lord with gladness
and come before his presence with a song.
Know this: the Lord himself is God;
he himself has made us, and we are his;
we are his people and the sheep of his pasture.
Enter his gates with thanksgiving;
go into his courts with praise;
give thanks to him and call upon his Name.
For the Lord is good;
his mercy is everlasting;
and his faithfulness endures from age to age.

During the first week of Easter, the Pascha Nostrum will be used in place of the Invitatory Psalm. It is appropriate to use this canticle throughout Eastertide.

Pascha Nostrum *Christ our Passover*

1 Corinthians 5:7-8; Romans 6:9-11; 1 Corinthians 15:20-22

Alleluia. Christ our Passover has been sacrificed for us;
therefore let us keep the feast,
Not with the old leaven, the leaven of malice and evil,
but with the unleavened bread of sincerity and truth. Alleluia.
Christ being raised from the dead will never die again;

death no longer has dominion over him.
The death that he died, he died to sin, once for all;
  but the life he lives, he lives to God.
So also consider yourselves dead to sin,
  and alive to God in Jesus Christ our Lord. Alleluia.
Christ has been raised from the dead,
  the first fruits of those who have fallen asleep.
For since by a man came death,
  by a man has come also the resurrection of the dead.
For as in Adam all die,
  so also in Christ shall all be made alive. Alleluia.

Then follows

The Psalm or Psalms Appointed

At the end of the Psalms is sung or said

Glory to the Father, and to the Son, and to the Holy Spirit;
  as it was in the beginning, is now, and ever shall be,
  world without end. Amen.

The Lessons

One or more Lessons, as appointed, are read, the Reader first saying

A Reading from _____.

A citation giving chapter and verse may be added.

After each Lesson the Reader may say

          The Word of the Lord.
People   Thanks be to God.

Or the Reader may say

          Here ends the Reading.

The following Canticles are normally sung or said after each of the lessons. The Officiant may also use a Canticle drawn from those on pages 35-43 or an appropriate song of praise.

Te Deum Laudamus   *We Praise You, O God*

We praise you, O God,
    we acclaim you as Lord;
    all creation worships you,
    the Father everlasting.
To you all angels, all the powers of heaven,
The cherubim and seraphim, sing in endless praise:
    Holy, Holy, Holy, Lord God of power and might,
    heaven and earth are full of your glory.
The glorious company of apostles praise you.
The noble fellowship of prophets praise you.
The white-robed army of martyrs praise you.
Throughout the world the holy Church acclaims you:
    Father, of majesty unbounded,
    your true and only Son, worthy of all praise,
    the Holy Spirit, advocate and guide.
You, Christ, are the king of glory,
    the eternal Son of the Father.
When you took our flesh to set us free
    you humbly chose the Virgin's womb.
You overcame the sting of death
    and opened the kingdom of heaven to all believers.
You are seated at God's right hand in glory.
    We believe that you will come to be our judge.

Come then, Lord, and help your people,
    bought with the price of your own blood,
    and bring us with your saints
    to glory everlasting.

Save your people, Lord, and bless your inheritance;
    govern and uphold them now and always.
Day by day we bless you;
    we praise your name forever.

Keep us today, Lord, from all sin;
>   have mercy on us, Lord, have mercy.
Lord, show us your love and mercy,
>   for we have put our trust in you.
In you, Lord, is our hope,
>   let us never be put to shame.

During Lent the Benedictus es, Domine usually replaces the Te Deum. The Benedictus es, Domine may be used at other times as well.

Benedictus es, Domine   *A Song of Praise*

Song of the Three Young Men, 29-34

Glory to you, Lord God of our fathers;
>   you are worthy of praise; glory to you.
Glory to you for the radiance of your holy Name;
>   we will praise you and highly exalt you for ever.
Glory to you in the splendor of your temple;
>   on the throne of your majesty, glory to you.
Glory to you, seated between the Cherubim;
>   we will praise you and highly exalt you for ever.
Glory to you, beholding the depths;
>   in the high vault of heaven, glory to you.
Glory to the Father, and to the Son, and to the Holy Spirit;
>   we will praise you and highly exalt you for ever.

Benedictus   *The Song of Zechariah*

Luke 1:68-79

Blessed be the Lord, the God of Israel;
>   he has come to his people and set them free.
He has raised up for us a mighty savior,
>   born of the house of his servant David.
Through his holy prophets he promised of old,
that he would save us from our enemies,
>   from the hands of all who hate us.

He promised to show mercy to our fathers
    and to remember his holy covenant.
This was the oath he swore to our father Abraham,
    to set us free from the hands of our enemies,
Free to worship him without fear,
    holy and righteous in his sight
    all the days of our life.
You, my child, shall be called the prophet of the Most High,
    for you will go before the Lord to prepare his way,
To give his people knowledge of salvation
    by the forgiveness of their sins.
In the tender compassion of our God
    the dawn from on high shall break upon us,
To shine on those who dwell in darkness and the shadow of death,
    and to guide our feet into the way of peace.
Glory to the Father, and to the Son, and to the Holy Spirit;
    as it was in the beginning, is now, and ever shall be,
    world without end. Amen.

If desired, a sermon on the Morning Lessons may be preached.

The Apostles' Creed

Officiant and People together, all standing

I believe in God, the Father almighty,
    creator of heaven and earth.
I believe in Jesus Christ, his only Son, our Lord.
    He was conceived by the Holy Spirit
    and born of the Virgin Mary.
    He suffered under Pontius Pilate,
    was crucified, died, and was buried.
    He descended to the dead.
    On the third day he rose again.
    He ascended into heaven,
    and is seated at the right hand of the Father.
    He will come again to judge the living and the dead.

I believe in the Holy Spirit,
    the holy catholic Church,
    the communion of saints,
    the forgiveness of sins,
    the resurrection of the body,
    and the life everlasting. Amen.

The Prayers

The People kneel or stand.

Officiant	The Lord be with you.
People	And with your spirit.
Officiant	Let us pray.

Lord, have mercy [upon us].
Christ, have mercy [upon us].
Lord, have mercy [upon us].

Officiant and People

Our Father, who art in heaven, hallowed be thy Name.
Thy kingdom come, thy will be done, on earth as it is in heaven.
Give us this day our daily bread.
And forgive us our trespasses, as we forgive those who trespass
    against us.
And lead us not into temptation, but deliver us from evil.
For thine is the kingdom, and the power, and the glory,
    forever and ever. Amen.

or this

Our Father in heaven, hallowed be your Name.
Your kingdom come, your will be done, on earth as it is in heaven.
Give us today our daily bread.
And forgive us our sins as we forgive those who sin against us.
Save us from the time of trial, and deliver us from evil.
For the kingdom, the power, and the glory are yours,
    now and forever. Amen.

Officiant	O Lord, show us your mercy;
People	And grant us your salvation.
Officiant	O Lord, save our nations;
People	And guide us in the way of justice and truth.
Officiant	Clothe your ministers with righteousness;
People	And make your chosen people joyful.
Officiant	O Lord, save your people;
People	And bless your inheritance.
Officiant	Give peace in our time, O Lord;
People	For only in you can we live in safety.
Officiant	Let not the needy, O Lord, be forgotten;
People	Nor the hope of the poor be taken away.
Officiant	Create in us clean hearts, O God;
People	And take not your Holy Spirit from us.

The Officiant then prays one or more of the following collects. It is traditional to pray the Collects for Peace and Grace daily. Alternatively, one may pray the collects on a weekly rotation, using the suggestions in parentheses.

The Collect of the Day

A Collect for Strength to Await Christ's Return (Sunday)

O God our King, by the resurrection of your Son Jesus Christ on the first day of the week, you conquered sin, put death to flight, and gave us the hope of everlasting life: Redeem all our days by this victory; forgive our sins, banish our fears, make us bold to praise you and to do your will; and steel us to wait for the consummation of your kingdom on the last great Day; through the same Jesus Christ our Lord. *Amen.*

A Collect for the Renewal of Life (Monday)

O God, the King eternal, whose light divides the day from the night and turns the shadow of death into the morning: Drive far from us all wrong desires, incline our hearts to keep your law, and guide our feet into the way of peace; that, having done your will with cheerfulness during the day, we may, when night comes, rejoice to give you thanks; through Jesus Christ our Lord. *Amen.*

A Collect for Peace (Tuesday)

O God, the author of peace and lover of concord, to know you is eternal life and to serve you is perfect freedom: Defend us, your humble servants, in all assaults of our enemies; that we, surely trusting in your defense, may not fear the power of any adversaries, through the might of Jesus Christ our Lord. *Amen.*

A Collect for Grace (Wednesday)

O Lord, our heavenly Father, almighty and everlasting God, you have brought us safely to the beginning of this day: Defend us by your mighty power, that we may not fall into sin nor run into any danger; and that guided by your Spirit, we may do what is righteous in your sight; through Jesus Christ our Lord. *Amen.*

A Collect for Guidance (Thursday)

Heavenly Father, in you we live and move and have our being: We humbly pray you so to guide and govern us by your Holy Spirit, that in all the cares and occupations of our life we may not forget you, but may remember that we are ever walking in your sight; through Jesus Christ our Lord. *Amen.*

A Collect for Endurance (Friday)

Almighty God, whose most dear Son went not up to joy but first he suffered pain, and entered not into glory before he was crucified: Mercifully grant that we, walking in the way of the cross, may find it none other than the way of life and peace; through Jesus Christ your Son our Lord. *Amen.*

A Collect for Sabbath Rest (Saturday)

Almighty God, who after the creation of the world rested from all your works and sanctified a day of rest for all your creatures: Grant that we, putting away all earthly anxieties, may be duly prepared for the service of your sanctuary, and that our rest here upon earth may be a preparation for the eternal rest promised to your people in heaven; through Jesus Christ our Lord. *Amen.*

Unless The Great Litany or the Eucharist is to follow, one of the following prayers for mission is added.

Almighty and everlasting God, who alone works great marvels: Send down upon our clergy and the congregations committed to their charge the life-giving Spirit of your grace, shower them with the continual dew of your blessing, and ignite in them a zealous love of your Gospel, through Jesus Christ our Lord. *Amen.*

O God, you have made of one blood all the peoples of the earth, and sent your blessed Son to preach peace to those who are far off and to those who are near: Grant that people everywhere may seek after you and find you; bring the nations into your fold; pour out your Spirit upon all flesh; and hasten the coming of your kingdom; through Jesus Christ our Lord. *Amen.*

Lord Jesus Christ, you stretched out your arms of love on the hard wood of the cross that everyone might come within the reach of your saving embrace: So clothe us in your Spirit that we, reaching forth our hands in love, may bring those who do not know you to the knowledge and love of you; for the honor of your Name. *Amen.*

Here may be sung a hymn or anthem.

The Officiant may invite the People to offer intercessions and thanksgivings.

Before the close of the Office one or both of the following may be used.

The General Thanksgiving

Officiant and People

Almighty God, Father of all mercies,
we your unworthy servants give you humble thanks
for all your goodness and loving-kindness
    to us and to all whom you have made.
We bless you for our creation, preservation,
    and all the blessings of this life;
but above all for your immeasurable love
in the redemption of the world by our Lord Jesus Christ;
for the means of grace, and for the hope of glory.
And, we pray, give us such an awareness of your mercies,
that with truly thankful hearts we may show forth your praise,
not only with our lips, but in our lives,
by giving up our selves to your service,
and by walking before you
    in holiness and righteousness all our days;
through Jesus Christ our Lord,
to whom, with you and the Holy Spirit,
be honor and glory throughout all ages. Amen.

A Prayer of St. John Chrysostom

Almighty God, you have given us grace at this time with one accord to make our common supplications to you; and you have promised through your well beloved Son that when two or three are gathered together in his name you will be in the midst of them: Fulfill now, O Lord, our desires and petitions as may be best for us; granting us in this world knowledge of your truth, and in the age to come life everlasting. *Amen.*

Officiant   Let us bless the Lord.
People   Thanks be to God.

From Easter Day through the Day of Pentecost "Alleluia, alleluia" may be added to the preceding versicle and response.

14 *Daily Morning Prayer*

The Officiant may invite the People to join in one of the Graces.

Officiant

The grace of our Lord Jesus Christ, and the love of God, and the fellowship of the Holy Spirit, be with us all evermore. *Amen.*
2 Corinthians 13:14

May the God of hope fill us with all joy and peace in believing through the power of the Holy Spirit. *Amen.*
Romans 15:13

Glory to God whose power, working in us, can do infinitely more than we can ask or imagine: Glory to him from generation to generation in the Church, and in Christ Jesus forever and ever. *Amen.*
Ephesians 3:20-21

Opening Sentences of Scripture

Advent

In the wilderness prepare the way of the Lord; make straight in the desert a highway for our God.
Isaiah 40:3

Christmas

Fear not, for behold, I bring you good news of a great joy that will be for all people. For unto you is born this day in the city of David a Savior, who is Christ the Lord.
Luke 2:10-11

Epiphany

For from the rising of the sun to its setting my name will be great among the nations, and in every place incense will be offered to my name, and a pure offering. For my name will be great among the nations, says the Lord of hosts.
Malachi 1:11

Lent

Repent, for the kingdom of heaven is at hand.
Matthew 3:2

Good Friday

Is it nothing to you, all you who pass by? Look and see if there is any sorrow like my sorrow, which was brought upon me, which the Lord inflicted on the day of his fierce anger.
Lamentations 1:12

Easter

Christ is risen! The Lord is risen indeed!
Mark 16:6 and Luke 24:34

Ascension

Since then we have a great high priest who has passed through the heavens, Jesus, the Son of God, let us hold fast our confession. Let us then with confidence draw near to the throne of grace, that we may receive mercy and find grace to help in time of need.
Hebrews 4:14, 16

Pentecost

You will receive power when the Holy Spirit has come upon you, and you will be my witnesses in Jerusalem and in all Judea and Samaria, and to the end of the earth.
Acts 1:8

Trinity Sunday

Holy, holy, holy, is the Lord God Almighty, who was and is and is to come!
Revelation 4:8

Days of Thanksgiving

Honor the Lord with your wealth and with the firstfruits of all your produce; then your barns will be filled with plenty, and your vats will be bursting with wine.
Proverbs 3:9-10

At any time

The Lord is in his holy temple; let all the earth keep silence before him.
Habakkuk 2:20

I was glad when they said to me, "Let us go to the house of the Lord!"
Psalm 122:1

Let the words of my mouth and the meditation of my heart be acceptable in your sight, O Lord, my rock and my redeemer.
Psalm 19:14

Send out your light and your truth; let them lead me; let them bring me to your holy hill and to your dwelling!
Psalm 43:3

For thus says the One who is high and lifted up, who inhabits eternity, whose name is Holy: "I dwell in the high and holy place, and also with him who is of a contrite and lowly spirit, to revive the spirit of the lowly, and to revive the heart of the contrite."
Isaiah 57:15

The hour is coming, and is now here, when the true worshipers will worship the Father in spirit and truth, for the Father is seeking such people to worship him.
John 4:23

Grace to you and peace from God our Father and the Lord Jesus Christ.
Philippians 1:2

General Instructions: Morning and Evening Prayer

The Confession and Apostles' Creed may be omitted, provided they have been said once during the course of the day.

In the opening versicles, the Officiant and People may join in saying "Alleluia" (outside of Lent) as an alternative to the versicles "Praise the Lord/The Lord's name be praised."

The following form of the Gloria Patri may be used:

> *Glory to the Father, and to the Son, and to the Holy Spirit:*
> *As it was in the beginning, is now, and will be forever. Amen.*

A sermon may also be preached after the Office or after the hymn or anthem (if sung) following the collects.

Daily Evening Prayer

Approved for Provincial Use

The Anglican Church in North America

Petertide, A.D. 2013

The Officiant may begin Evening Prayer by reading an opening sentence of Scripture found on pages 31-33 or another appropriate Scripture. The Confession of Sin may be said, or the Office may continue with "O Lord, open our lips."

Confession of Sin

The Officiant says to the People

Dearly beloved, the Scriptures teach us to acknowledge our many sins and offenses, not concealing them from our heavenly Father, but confessing them with humble and obedient hearts that we may obtain forgiveness by his infinite goodness and mercy. We ought at all times humbly to acknowledge our sins before Almighty God, but especially when we come together in his presence to give thanks for the great benefits we have received at his hands, to declare his most worthy praise, to hear his holy Word, and to ask, for ourselves and others, those things necessary for our life and our salvation. Therefore, come with me to the throne of heavenly grace.

or this

Let us humbly confess our sins to Almighty God.

Silence is kept. All kneeling the Officiant and People say

Almighty and most merciful Father,
we have erred and strayed from your ways like lost sheep.
we have followed too much the deceits and desires of our
        own hearts.

we have offended against your holy laws.
we have left undone those things which we ought to
    have done,
and we have done those things which we ought not to
    have done;
and apart from your grace, there is no health in us.
O Lord, have mercy upon us.
Spare those who confess their faults.
Restore those who are penitent, according to your promises declared
    to all people in Christ Jesus our Lord;
And grant, O most merciful Father, for his sake,
    that we may now live a godly, righteous, and sober life,
    to the glory of your holy Name. Amen.

The Priest alone stands and says

Almighty God, the Father of our Lord Jesus Christ, desires not the
death of sinners, but that they may turn from their wickedness and
live. He has empowered and commanded his ministers to pronounce
to his people, being penitent, the absolution and remission of their
sins. He pardons all who truly repent and genuinely believe his holy
Gospel. For this reason, we beseech him to grant us true repentance
and his Holy Spirit, that our present deeds may please him, the rest of
our lives may be pure and holy, and that at the last we may come to
his eternal joy; through Jesus Christ our Lord. *Amen.*

or this

The Almighty and merciful Lord grant you absolution and remission
of all your sins, true repentance, amendment of life, and the grace
and consolation of his Holy Spirit. *Amen.*

A deacon or layperson remains kneeling and prays

Grant your faithful people, merciful Lord, pardon and peace; that we
may be cleansed from all our sins, and serve you with a quiet mind;
through Jesus Christ our Lord. *Amen.*

The Invitatory

All stand

Officiant	O Lord, open our lips.
People	And our mouth shall proclaim your praise.
Officiant	O God, make speed to save us;
People	O Lord, make haste to help us.
Officiant	Glory to the Father, and to the Son, and to the Holy Spirit;
People	As it was in the beginning, is now, and ever shall be, world without end. Amen.
Officiant	Praise the Lord.
People	The Lord's name be praised.

The following or some other suitable hymn or Psalm may be sung or said

Phos hilaron   *O Gladsome Light*

O gladsome light,
pure brightness of the ever-living Father in heaven,
O Jesus Christ, holy and blessed!
Now as we come to the setting of the sun,
and our eyes behold the vesper light,
we sing praises to God: the Father, the Son, and the Holy Spirit.
You are worthy at all times to be praised by happy voices,
O Son of God, O Giver of Life,
and to be glorified through all the worlds.

Then follows

The Psalm or Psalms Appointed

At the end of the Psalms is sung or said

Glory to the Father, and to the Son, and to the Holy Spirit;
as it was in the beginning, is now, and ever shall be,
world without end. Amen.

The Lessons

One or more Lessons, as appointed, are read, the Reader first saying

A Reading from _____ .

A citation giving chapter and verse may be added.

After each Lesson the Reader may say

The Word of the Lord.
People   Thanks be to God.

Or the Reader may say

Here ends the Reading.

The following Canticles are normally sung or said after each of the lessons. The Officiant may also use a Canticle drawn from those on pages 35-43 or an appropriate song of praise.

Magnificat   *The Song of Mary*

Luke 1:46-55

My soul magnifies the Lord,
    and my spirit rejoices in God my Savior.
For he has regarded
    the lowliness of his handmaiden.
For behold, from now on,
    all generations will call me blessed.
For he that is mighty has magnified me,
    and holy is his Name.
And his mercy is on those who fear him,
    throughout all generations.
He has shown the strength of his arm;
    he has scattered the proud in the imagination of their hearts.
He has brought down the mighty from their thrones,
    and has exalted the humble and meek.
He has filled the hungry with good things,
    and the rich he has sent empty away.

He, remembering his mercy, has helped his servant Israel,
    as he promised to our fathers, Abraham and his seed forever.
Glory to the Father, and to the Son, and to the Holy Spirit;
    as it was in the beginning, is now, and ever shall be,
    world without end. Amen.

Nunc dimittis   *The Song of Simeon*

Luke 2:29-32

Lord, now let your servant depart in peace,
    according to your word.
For my eyes have seen your salvation,
    which you have prepared before the face of all people;
to be a light to lighten the Gentiles,
    and to be the glory of your people Israel.
Glory to the Father, and to the Son, and to the Holy Spirit;
    as it was in the beginning, is now, and ever shall be, world
    without end. Amen.

If desired, a sermon on the Evening Lessons may be preached.

The Apostles' Creed

Officiant and People together, all standing

I believe in God, the Father almighty,
    creator of heaven and earth.
I believe in Jesus Christ, his only Son, our Lord.
    He was conceived by the Holy Spirit
    and born of the Virgin Mary.
    He suffered under Pontius Pilate,
    was crucified, died, and was buried.
    He descended to the dead.
    On the third day he rose again.
    He ascended into heaven,
    and is seated at the right hand of the Father.
    He will come again to judge the living and the dead.

I believe in the Holy Spirit,
the holy catholic Church,
the communion of saints,
the forgiveness of sins,
the resurrection of the body,
and the life everlasting. Amen.

The Prayers

The People kneel or stand.

Officiant	The Lord be with you.
People	And with your spirit.
Officiant	Let us pray.

Lord, have mercy [upon us].
Christ, have mercy [upon us].
Lord, have mercy [upon us].

Officiant and People

Our Father, who art in heaven, hallowed be thy Name.
Thy kingdom come, thy will be done, on earth as it is in heaven.
Give us this day our daily bread.
And forgive us our trespasses, as we forgive those who trespass
against us.
And lead us not into temptation, but deliver us from evil.
For thine is the kingdom, and the power, and the glory,
forever and ever. Amen.

or this

Our Father in heaven, hallowed be your Name.
Your kingdom come, your will be done, on earth as it is in heaven.
Give us today our daily bread.
And forgive us our sins as we forgive those who sin against us.
Save us from the time of trial, and deliver us from evil.
For the kingdom, the power, and the glory are yours,
now and forever. Amen.

Officiant	O Lord, show us your mercy;
People	And grant us your salvation.
Officiant	O Lord, save our nations;
People	And guide us in the way of justice and truth.
Officiant	Clothe your ministers with righteousness;
People	And make your chosen people joyful.
Officiant	O Lord, save your people;
People	And bless your inheritance.
Officiant	Give peace in our time, O Lord;
People	For only in you can we live in safety.
Officiant	Let not the needy, O Lord, be forgotten;
People	Nor the hope of the poor be taken away.
Officiant	Create in us clean hearts, O God;
People	And take not your Holy Spirit from us.

The Officiant then prays one or more of the following collects. It is traditional to pray the Collects for Peace and Aid against Perils daily. Alternatively, one may pray the collects on a weekly rotation, using the suggestions in parentheses.

The Collect of the Day

A Collect for Resurrection Hope (Sunday)

Lord God, whose Son our Savior Jesus Christ triumphed over the powers of death and prepared for us our place in the new Jerusalem: Grant that we, who have this day given thanks for his resurrection, may praise you in that City of which he is the light, and where he lives and reigns forever and ever. *Amen.*

A Collect for Peace (Monday)

O God, the source of all holy desires, all good counsels, and all just works: Give to your servants that peace which the world cannot give, that our hearts may be set to obey your commandments, and that we, being defended from the fear of our enemies, may pass our time in rest and quietness, through the merits of Jesus Christ our Savior. *Amen.*

A Collect for Aid against Perils (Tuesday)

Lighten our darkness, we beseech you, O Lord; and by your great mercy defend us from all perils and dangers of this night; for the love of your only Son, our Savior Jesus Christ. *Amen.*

A Collect for Protection (Wednesday)

O God, the life of all who live, the light of the faithful, the strength of those who labor, and the repose of the dead: We thank you for the blessings of the day that is past, and humbly ask for your protection through the coming night. Bring us in safety to the morning hours; through him who died and rose again for us, your Son our Savior Jesus Christ. *Amen.*

A Collect for the Presence of Christ (Thursday)

Lord Jesus, stay with us, for evening is at hand and the day is past; be our companion in the way, kindle our hearts, and awaken hope, that we may know you as you are revealed in Scripture and the breaking of bread. Grant this for the sake of your love. *Amen.*

A Collect for Faith (Friday)

Lord Jesus Christ, by your death you took away the sting of death: Grant to us your servants so to follow in faith where you have led the way, that we may at length fall asleep peacefully in you and wake up in your likeness; for your tender mercies' sake. *Amen.*

A Collect for the Eve of Worship (Saturday)

O God, the source of eternal light: Shed forth your unending day upon us who watch for you, that our lips may praise you, our lives may bless you, and our worship on the morrow give you glory; through Jesus Christ our Lord. *Amen.*

Unless the Eucharist is to follow, one of the following prayers for mission is added.

O God and Father of all, whom the whole heavens adore: Let the whole earth also worship you, all nations obey you, all tongues confess and bless you, and men, women and children everywhere love you and serve you in peace; through Jesus Christ our Lord. *Amen.*

Keep watch, dear Lord, with those who work, or watch, or weep this night, and give your angels charge over those who sleep. Tend the sick, Lord Christ; give rest to the weary, bless the dying, soothe the suffering, pity the afflicted, shield the joyous; and all for your love's sake. *Amen.*

O God, you manifest in your servants the signs of your presence: Send forth upon us the Spirit of love, that in companionship with one another your abounding grace may increase among us; through Jesus Christ our Lord. *Amen.*

Here may be sung a hymn or anthem.

The Officiant may invite the People to offer intercessions and thanksgivings.

Before the close of the Office one or both of the following may be used.

The General Thanksgiving

Officiant and People

Almighty God, Father of all mercies,
we your unworthy servants give you humble thanks
for all your goodness and loving-kindness
    to us and to all whom you have made.
We bless you for our creation, preservation,
    and all the blessings of this life;
but above all for your immeasurable love
in the redemption of the world by our Lord Jesus Christ;
for the means of grace, and for the hope of glory.
And, we pray, give us, such an awareness of your mercies,
that with truly thankful hearts we may show forth your praise,

not only with our lips, but in our lives,
by giving up our selves to your service,
and by walking before you
    in holiness and righteousness all our days;
through Jesus Christ our Lord,
to whom, with you and the Holy Spirit,
be honor and glory throughout all ages. Amen.

A Prayer of St. John Chrysostom

Almighty God, you have given us grace at this time with one accord
to make our common supplications to you; and you have promised
through your well beloved Son that when two or three are gathered
together in his name you will be in the midst of them: Fulfill now, O
Lord, our desires and petitions as may be best for us; granting us in
this world knowledge of your truth, and in the age to come life
everlasting. *Amen.*

Officiant	Let us bless the Lord.
People	Thanks be to God.

*From Easter Day through the Day of Pentecost "Alleluia, alleluia" may be added to the
preceding versicle and response. The Officiant may invite the People to join in praying one of
the graces given below.*

Officiant

The grace of our Lord Jesus Christ, and the love of God, and the
fellowship of the Holy Spirit, be with us all evermore. *Amen.*
2 Corinthians 13:14

May the God of hope fill us with all joy and peace in believing
through the power of the Holy Spirit. *Amen.*
Romans 15:13

Glory to God whose power, working in us, can do infinitely more
than we can ask or imagine: Glory to him from generation to
generation in the Church, and in Christ Jesus forever and ever. *Amen.*
Ephesians 3:20-21

Opening Sentences of Scripture

Advent

Therefore stay awake – for you do not know when the master of the house will come, in the evening, or at midnight, or when the cock crows, or in the morning – lest he come suddenly and find you asleep.
Mark 13:35-36

Christmas

Behold, the dwelling place of God is with man. He will dwell with them, and they will be his people, and God himself will be with them as their God.
Revelation 21:3

Epiphany

Nations shall come to your light, and kings to the brightness of your rising.
Isaiah 60:3

Lent

If we say we have no sin, we deceive ourselves, and the truth is not in us. If we confess our sins, he is faithful and just to forgive us our sins and to cleanse us from all unrighteousness.
1 John 1:8-9

For I know my transgressions, and my sin is ever before me.
Psalm 51:3

To the Lord our God belong mercy and forgiveness, for we have rebelled against him.
Daniel 9:9

Good Friday

All we like sheep have gone astray; we have turned every one to his own way; and the Lord has laid on him the iniquity of us all.
Isaiah 53:6

Easter

Thanks be to God, who gives us the victory through our Lord Jesus Christ.
1 Corinthians 15:57

If then you have been raised with Christ, seek the things that are above, where Christ is, seated at the right hand of God.
Colossians 3:1

Ascension

For Christ has entered, not into holy places made with hands, which are copies of the true things, but into heaven itself, now to appear in the presence of God on our behalf.
Hebrews 9:24

Pentecost

The Spirit and the Bride say, "Come." And let the one who hears say, "Come." And let the one who is thirsty come; let the one who desires take the water of life without price.
Revelation 22:17

There is a river whose streams make glad the city of God, the holy habitation of the Most High.
Psalm 46:4

Trinity Sunday

Holy, holy, holy, is the Lord God of Hosts; the whole earth is full of his glory!
Isaiah 6:3

Days of Thanksgiving

The Lord by wisdom founded the earth; by understanding he established the heavens; by his knowledge the deeps broke open, and the clouds drop down the dew.
Proverbs 3:19-20

At any time

The Lord is in his holy temple; let all the earth keep silence before him.
Habakkuk 2:20

O Lord, I love the habitation of your house and the place where your glory dwells.
Psalm 46:8

Let my prayer be counted as incense before you, and the lifting up of my hands as the evening sacrifice!
Psalm 141:2

Worship the Lord in the splendor of holiness; tremble before him, all the earth!
Psalm 96:9

Let the words of my mouth and the meditation of my heart be acceptable in your sight, O Lord, my rock and my redeemer.
Psalm 19:14

General Instructions: Morning and Evening Prayer

The Confession and Apostles' Creed may be omitted, provided they have been said once during the course of the day.

In the opening versicles, the Officiant and People may join in saying "Alleluia" (outside of Lent) as an alternative to the versicles "Praise the Lord/The Lord's name be praised."

The following form of the Gloria Patri may be used:

> *Glory to the Father, and to the Son, and to the Holy Spirit:*
> *As it was in the beginning, is now, and will be forever. Amen.*

A sermon may also be preached after the Office or after the hymn or anthem (if sung) following the collects.

Supplemental Canticles

for Worship

Approved for Provincial Use

The Anglican Church in North America

Petertide, A.D. 2013

Especially suitable for use in Advent and Easter

Magna et mirabilia   *The Song of the Redeemed*

Revelation 15:3-4

O ruler of the universe, Lord God,
    great deeds are they that you have done,
    surpassing human understanding.
Your ways are ways of righteousness and truth,
    O King of all the ages.
Who can fail to do you homage, Lord,
    and sing the praises of your Name?
    for you only are the Holy One.
All nations will draw near and fall down before you,
    because your just and holy works have been revealed.
Glory to the Father, and to the Son, and to the Holy Spirit;
    as it was in the beginning, is now, and ever shall be, world
    without end. Amen.

Especially suitable for use during the season after Epiphany

Surge, illuminare   *Arise, shine, for your light has come*

Isaiah 60:1-3, 11a, 14c, 18-19

Arise, shine, for you light has come,
    and the glory of the Lord has dawned upon you.

For behold, darkness covers the land;
  deep gloom enshrouds the peoples.
But over you the Lord will rise,
  and his glory will appear upon you.
Nations will stream to your light,
  and kings to the brightness of your dawning.
Your gates will always be open;
  by day or night they will never be shut.
They will call you, The City of the Lord,
  the Zion of the Holy One of Israel.
Violence will no more be heard in your land,
  ruin or destruction within your borders.
You will call your walls, Salvation,
  and all your portals, Praise.
The sun will no more be your light by day;
  by night you will not need the brightness of the moon.
The Lord will be your everlasting light,
  and your God will be your glory.
Glory to the Father, and to the Son, and to the Holy Spirit;
  as it was in the beginning, is now, and ever shall be,
  world without end. Amen.

Especially suitable for use during Lent

Kyrie Pantokrator *A Song of Penitence*

Prayer of Manasseh, 1-2, 4, 6-7, 11-15

O Lord and Ruler of the hosts of heaven,
  God of Abraham, Isaac, and Jacob,
  and of all their righteous offspring:
You made the heavens and the earth,
  with all their vast array.
All things quake with fear at your presence;
  they tremble because of your power.
But your merciful promise is beyond all measure;

it surpasses all that our minds can fathom.
O Lord, you are full of compassion,
    long-suffering, and abounding in mercy.
You hold back your hand;
    you do not punish as we deserve.
In your great goodness, Lord,
    you have promised forgiveness to sinners,
    that they may repent of their sin and be saved.
And now, O Lord, I bend the knee of my heart,
    and make my appeal, sure of your gracious goodness.
I have sinned, O Lord, I have sinned,
    and I know my wickedness only too well.
Therefore I make this prayer to you:
    Forgive me, Lord, forgive me.
Do not let me perish in my sin,
    nor condemn me to the depths of the earth.
For you, O Lord, are the God of those who repent,
    and in me you will show forth your goodness.
Unworthy as I am, you will save me,
    in accordance with your great mercy,
    and I will praise you without ceasing all the days of my life.
For all the powers of heaven sing your praises,
    and yours is the glory to ages of ages. Amen.

Especially suitable for use during Lent

Quaerite Dominum   *Seek the Lord while he wills to be found*

Isaiah 55:6-11

Seek the Lord while he wills to be found;
    call upon him when he draws near.
Let the wicked forsake their ways
    and the evil ones their thoughts;
And let them turn to the Lord, and he will have compassion,
    and to our God, for he will richly pardon.

For my thoughts are not your thoughts,
    nor your ways my ways, says the Lord.
For as the heavens are higher than the earth,
    so are my ways higher than your ways,
    and my thoughts than your thoughts.
For as rain and snow fall form the heavens
    and return not again, but water the earth,
Bringing forth life and giving growth,
    seed for sowing and bread for eating,
So is my word that goes forth from my mouth;
    it will not return to me empty;
But it will accomplish that which I have purposed,
    and prosper in that for which I sent it.
Glory to the Father, and to the Son, and to the Holy Spirit;
    as it was in the beginning, is now, and ever shall be, world
    without end. Amen.

Especially suitable for use in Easter

Cantemus Domino   *The Song of Moses*

Exodus 15:1-6, 11-13, 17-18

I will sing to the Lord, for he is lofty and uplifted;
    the horse and its rider has he hurled into the sea.
The Lord is my strength and my refuge;
    the Lord has become my Savior.
This is my God and I will praise him,
    the God of my people and I will exalt him.
The Lord is a mighty warrior;
    Yahweh is his Name.
The chariots of Pharaoh and his army has he hurled into the sea;
    the finest of those who bear armor have been drowned in the
    Red Sea.
The fathomless deep has overwhelmed them;
    they sank into the depths like a stone.

Your right hand, O Lord, is glorious in might;
    your right hand, O Lord, has overthrown the enemy.
Who can be compared with you, O Lord, among the gods?
    who is like you, glorious in holiness,
    awesome in renown, and worker of wonders?
Your stretched forth your right hand;
    the earth swallowed them up.
With your constant love you led the people you redeemed;
    you brought them in safety to your holy dwelling.
You will bring them in and plant them
    on the mount of your possession,
The resting-place you have made for yourself, O Lord,
    the sanctuary, O Lord, that your hand has established.
The Lord shall reign for ever and for ever.
Glory to the Father, and to the Son, and to the Holy Spirit;
    as it was in the beginning, is now, and ever shall be,
    world without end. Amen.

Especially suitable for use after Ascension and in Easter season

Dignus es   *A Song to the Lamb*

Revelation 4:11; 5:9-10, 13

Splendor and honor and kingly power
    are yours by right, O Lord our God,
For you created everything that is,
    and by your will they were created and have their being;
And yours by right, O Lamb that was slain,
    for with your blood you have redeemed for God,
From every family, language, people and nation,
    a kingdom of priests to serve our God.
And so, to him who sits upon the throne,
    and to Christ the Lamb,
Be worship and praise, dominion and splendor,
    for ever and for evermore.

Cantate Domino *Sing to the Lord a New Song*

Psalm 98

Sing to the Lord a new song,
  for he has done marvelous things.
With his right hand and his holy arm
  has he won for himself the victory.
The Lord has made known his victory;
  his righteousness has he openly shown in the sight of the nations.
He remembers his mercy and faithfulness to the house of Israel,
  and all the ends of the earth have seen the victory of our God.
Shout with joy to the Lord, all you lands; lift up your voice, rejoice,
  and sing.
Sing to the Lord with the harp,
  with the harp and the voice of song.
With trumpets and the sound of the horn
  shout with joy before the King, the Lord.
Let the sea make a noise and all that is in it,
  the lands and those who dwell therein.
Let the rivers clap their hands,
  and let the hills ring out with joy before the Lord,
  when he comes to judge the earth.
In righteousness shall he judge the world
  and the peoples with equity.
Glory to the Father, and to the Son, and to the Holy Spirit;
  as it was in the beginning, is now, and ever shall be,
  world without end. Amen.

Suitable for use at any time

Ecce, Deus *Surely, it is God who saves me*

Isaiah 12:2-6

Surely, it is God who saves me;
  I will trust in him and not be afraid.

For the Lord is my stronghold and my sure defense,
    and he will be my Savior.
Therefore you shall draw water with rejoicing
    from the springs of salvation.
And on that day you shall say,
    Give thanks to the Lord and call upon his Name;
Make his deeds known among the peoples;
    see that they remember that his Name is exalted.
Sing the praises of the Lord, for he has done great things,
    and this is known in all the world.
Cry aloud, inhabitants of Zion, ring out your joy,
    for the great one in the midst of you is the Holy One of Israel.
Glory to the Father, and to the Son, and to the Holy Spirit;
    as it was in the beginning, is now, and ever shall be,
    world without end. Amen.

Suitable for use at any time

Deus misereatur   *May God be Merciful to us and Bless us*

Psalm 67

May God be merciful to us and bless us,
    show us the light of his countenance and come to us.
Let your ways be known upon earth,
    your saving health among all nations.
Let the peoples praise you, O God;
    let all the peoples praise you.
Let the nations be glad and sing for joy,
    for you judge the peoples with equity and guide all the nations
    upon earth.
Let the peoples praise you, O God;
    let all the peoples praise you.
The earth has brought forth her increase;
    may God, our own God, give us his blessing.
May God give us his blessing,

and may all the ends of the earth stand in awe of him.
Glory to the Father, and to the Son, and to the Holy Spirit;
   as it was in the beginning, is now, and ever shall be,
   world without end. Amen.

Especially suitable for use on Saturday

Benedicite, omnia opera Domini   *A Song of Creation*

Song of the Three Young Men, 35-65

Invocation

Glorify the Lord, all you works of the Lord,
   praise him and highly exalt him for ever.
In the firmament of his power, glorify the Lord,
   praise him and highly exalt him for ever.

I The Cosmic Order

Glorify the Lord, you angels and all powers of the Lord,
   O heavens and all waters above the heavens.
Sun and moon and stars of the sky, glorify the Lord,
   praise him and highly exalt him for ever.

Glorify the Lord, every shower of rain and fall of dew,
   all winds and fire and heat,
Winter and summer, glorify the Lord,
   praise him and highly exalt him for ever.

Glorify the Lord, O chill and cold,
   drops of dew and flakes of snow.
Frost and cold, ice and sleet, glorify the Lord,
   praise him and highly exalt him for ever.

Glorify the Lord, of nights and days,
   O shining light and enfolding dark.
Storm clouds and thunderbolts, glorify the Lord,
   praise him and highly exalt him for ever.

II *The Earth and its Creatures*

Let the earth glorify the Lord,
    praise him and highly exalt him forever.
Glorify the Lord, O mountains and hills,
    and all that grows upon the earth,
    praise him and highly exalt him forever.
Glorify the Lord, O springs of water, seas, and streams,
    O whales and all that move in the waters.
All birds of the air, glorify the Lord,
    praise him and highly exalt him forever.

Glorify the Lord, O beasts of the wild,
    and all you flocks and herds.
O men and women everywhere, glorify the Lord,
    praise him and highly exalt him forever.

III *The People of God*

Let the people of God glorify the Lord,
    praise him and highly exalt him forever.
Glorify the Lord, O priests and servants of the Lord,
    praise him and highly exalt him forever.

Glorify the Lord, O spirits and souls of the righteous,
    praise him and highly exalt him forever.
You that are holy and humble of heart, glorify the Lord,
    praise him and highly exalt him forever.

Doxology

Let us glorify the Lord: the Father, the Son and the Holy Spirit;
    praise him and highly exalt him forever.
In the firmament of his power, glorify the Lord,
    praise him and highly exalt him forever.

The Order for the Administration of

The Lord's Supper

or

Holy Communion,

commonly called

The Holy Eucharist

Long Form

Approved for Provincial Use

The Anglican Church in North America

Petertide, A.D. 2013

A hymn, psalm, or anthem may be sung.

The Acclamation

The People standing, the Celebrant says this or a seasonal greeting as found on pages 62-63.

	Blessed be God, the Father, the Son and the Holy Spirit.
People	And blessed be his kingdom, now and forever. Amen.

In place of the above, from Easter Day through the Day of Pentecost

Celebrant	Alleluia. Christ is risen.
People	The Lord is risen indeed. Alleluia.

The Collect for Purity

The Celebrant prays (and the People may be invited to join)

Almighty God, to you all hearts are open, all desires known, and
from you no secrets are hid: Cleanse the thoughts of our hearts by
the inspiration of your Holy Spirit, that we may perfectly love you,
and worthily magnify your holy Name; through Christ our Lord.
Amen.

The Summary of the Law

*The Celebrant then reads the Summary of the Law. The Decalogue may be used at any time
in place of the Summary of the Law. It is appropriate to use the Decalogue throughout the
seasons of Advent and Lent and on other penitential occasions.*

Jesus said: You shall love the Lord your God with all your heart and
with all your soul and with all your mind. This is the great and first
commandment. And a second is like it: You shall love your neighbor
as yourself. On these two commandments depend all the Law and
the Prophets.
Matthew 22:37-40

Kyrie

The Celebrant and people may sing or pray together once or three times

Lord, have mercy [upon us].	*or*	Kyrie eleison.
Christ, have mercy [upon us].		*Christe eleison.*
Lord, have mercy [upon us].		Kyrie eleison.

or this

Trisagion

Holy God,
Holy and Mighty,
Holy Immortal One,
Have mercy upon us.

Gloria in Excelsis

The Gloria or some other song of praise may be sung or said, all standing. It is appropriate to omit the song of praise during penitential seasons and days appointed for fasting. The Gloria may alternatively be placed immediately before the Blessing and Dismissal.

Glory to God in the highest,
    and peace to his people on earth.
Lord God, heavenly King,
almighty God and Father,
    we worship you, we give you thanks,
    we praise you for your glory.
Lord Jesus Christ, only Son of the Father,
Lord God, Lamb of God,
you take away the sin of the world:
    have mercy on us;
you are seated at the right hand of the Father:
    receive our prayer.
For you alone are the Holy One,
you alone are the Lord,
you alone are the Most High,
    Jesus Christ,
    with the Holy Spirit,
    in the glory of God the Father. Amen.

The Collect of the Day

The Celebrant says to the People

	The Lord be with you.
People	And with your spirit.
Celebrant	Let us pray.

The Celebrant prays the Collect. When concluded, the people respond praying

People	Amen.

The Lessons

One or more Lessons, as appointed, are read, the Reader first saying

A Reading from _____.

A citation giving chapter and verse may be added.

After each Lesson, the Reader may say

The Word of the Lord.
People   Thanks be to God.

Silence may follow.

A psalm, hymn or anthem may follow each reading.

All standing, the Deacon or Priest reads the Gospel, first saying

The Holy Gospel of our Lord Jesus Christ according
to _____.

People   Glory to you, Lord Christ.

After the Gospel, the Reader says

The Gospel of the Lord.
People   Praise to you, Lord Christ.

The Sermon

Nicene Creed

On Sundays, other Major Feast Days, and other times as appointed, all stand to recite the Nicene Creed, the Celebrant first saying

Let us confess our faith in the words of the Nicene Creed:

Celebrant and People

We believe in one God,
    the Father, the Almighty,
    maker of heaven and earth,
    of all that is, visible and invisible.

We believe in one Lord, Jesus Christ,
the only Son of God,
eternally begotten of the Father,
God from God, Light from Light,
true God from true God,
begotten, not made,
of one Being with the Father;
through him all things were made.
For us and for our salvation he came down from heaven,
was incarnate from the Holy Spirit and the Virgin Mary,
and was made man.
For our sake he was crucified under Pontius Pilate;
he suffered death and was buried.
On the third day he rose again in accordance with the Scriptures;
he ascended into heaven
and is seated at the right hand of the Father.
He will come again in glory to judge the living and the dead,
and his kingdom will have no end.

We believe in the Holy Spirit, the Lord, the giver of life,
who proceeds from the Father [and the Son]*,
who with the Father and the Son is worshiped and glorified,
who has spoken through the prophets.
We believe in one holy catholic and apostolic Church.
We acknowledge one baptism for the forgiveness of sins.
We look for the resurrection of the dead,
and the life of the world to come. Amen.

---

* The *filioque* [and the Son] is not in the original Greek text. Nevertheless, in the Western Church the *filioque* [and the Son] is customary at worship and is used for the explication of doctrine [*39 Articles of Religion*]. The operative resolution of the College of Bishops concerning use of the *filioque* is printed with the General Instructions at the end of the Holy Communion, Long Form.

The Prayers of the People

The Prayers, the Exhortation, the Confession and Absolution, the Comfortable Words and the Peace may alternatively be placed after the Offertory.

After each petition there is a time of silence for the Clergy and People to add their own prayers. Alternatively, the prayers may be read straight through by the Deacon or other person appointed, without pausing to pray, "Lord in your mercy, hear our prayer."

The Deacon or other person appointed says

Let us pray for the Church and for the world.

Almighty and ever-living God, we are taught by your holy Word to offer prayers and supplications and to give thanks for all people. We humbly pray that you would mercifully receive our prayers. Inspire continually, we pray, the universal Church with the spirit of truth, unity and concord; and grant that all who confess your holy Name may agree in the truth of your holy Word, and live in unity and godly love.

Silence

Reader	Lord, in your mercy.
People	Hear our prayer.

We pray that you will lead the nations of the world into the way of righteousness; and so guide and direct their leaders, especially *N,* our *President/Prime Minister/Sovereign,* that your people may enjoy the blessings of freedom and peace. Grant that our leaders may impartially administer justice, uphold integrity and truth, restrain wickedness and vice, and maintain true religion.

Silence

Reader	Lord, in your mercy.
People	Hear our prayer.

Give grace, heavenly Father, to all Bishops, Priests, and Deacons, *and especially to your servant(s) N, our Archbishop/Bishop/Priest/Deacon, etc.,* that by their life and teaching, they may proclaim your true and life-giving Word, and rightly and duly administer your holy Sacraments. And to all your people give your heavenly grace, and especially to this congregation, that with reverent and obedient hearts we may hear and receive your holy Word, and serve you in holiness and righteousness all the days of our lives.

Silence

Reader	Lord in your mercy.
People	Hear our prayer.

Prosper, we pray, all those who proclaim the Gospel of your kingdom among the nations, and help us to fulfill your great commission; making disciples of all nations; teaching them to obey all that you have commanded.

Silence

Reader	Lord in your mercy.
People	Hear our prayer.

We ask you in your goodness, Lord, to comfort and sustain all who in this transitory life are in trouble, sorrow, need, sickness, or any other adversity [especially _____].

Silence

Reader	Lord in your mercy.
People	Hear our prayer.

We remember before you Lord, all your servants departed this life in faith and fear: and we bless your holy Name for all who in life and death have glorified you; praying that you will give us grace that, rejoicing in their fellowship, we may follow their good examples, and with them be partakers of your heavenly kingdom.

Silence

Reader	Lord in your mercy.
People	Hear our prayer.

The Celebrant concludes with the following prayer

Heavenly Father, grant these our prayers for Jesus Christ's sake, our only Mediator and Advocate, who lives and reigns with you in the unity of the Holy Spirit, now and forever. *Amen.*

The Exhortation

It is customary for the Celebrant to say the Exhortation on the First Sunday in Advent, the First Sunday in Lent, and on Trinity Sunday.

The Confession and Absolution of Sin

The Deacon or other person appointed says the following

All who truly and earnestly repent of your sins, and seek to be reconciled with your neighbors, and intend to lead the new life, following the commandments of God, and walking in his holy ways: draw near with faith and make your humble confession to Almighty God.

Silence

The Deacon and People kneel as able and pray

Almighty God, Father of our Lord Jesus Christ,
maker and judge of us all:
We acknowledge and repent of our many sins and offenses,
which we have committed by thought, word, and deed,
    against your divine majesty,
provoking most justly your righteous anger against us.
We are deeply sorry for these transgressions.
The burden of them is more than we can bear.
Have mercy upon us, most merciful Father;
for your Son our Lord Jesus Christ's sake,
forgive us all that is past;
and grant that we may evermore serve and please you in newness of
    life,
to the honor and glory of your Name;
through Jesus Christ our Lord. Amen.

Almighty God, our heavenly Father, who in his great mercy has promised forgiveness of sins to all those who sincerely repent and with true faith turn to him, have mercy upon you, pardon and deliver you from all your sins, confirm and strengthen you in all goodness, and bring you to everlasting life; through Jesus Christ our Lord. *Amen.*

The Comfortable Words

The Celebrant may then say one or more of the following sentences, first saying

Hear the Word of God to all who truly turn to him.

Come to me, all who labor and are heavy laden, and I will give you rest.
Matthew 11:28

God so loved the world, that he gave his only-begotten Son, that whoever believes in him should not perish but have eternal life.
John 3:16

The saying is trustworthy and deserving of full acceptance, that Christ Jesus came into the world to save sinners.
1 Timothy 1:15

If anyone sins, we have an advocate with the Father, Jesus Christ the righteous. He is the propitiation for our sins, and not for ours only but also for the sins of the whole world.
1 John 2:1-2

The Peace

Celebrant	The Peace of the Lord be always with you.
People	And with your spirit.

Then the Ministers and People may greet one another in the name of the Lord.

The Offertory

The Celebrant may begin the Offertory with one of the provided sentences of Scripture.

During the Offertory a hymn, psalm, or anthem may be sung. The Deacon or Priest prepares the Holy Table for the celebration. Representatives of the congregation may bring the People's offerings of bread and wine, and money or other gifts, to the Deacon or Priest.

The People stand while the offerings are presented.

The Celebrant may pray the following prayer

Yours, O Lord, is the greatness, and the power, and the glory, and the victory, and the majesty: for everything in heaven and on earth is yours; yours is the Kingdom, O Lord, and you are exalted as Head above all. All things come from you, O Lord, and of your own have we given you.
1 Chronicles 29:11, 14

The Sursum Corda

The People remain standing. The Celebrant faces them and sings or says

	The Lord be with you.
People	And with your spirit.
Celebrant	Lift up your hearts.
People	We lift them to the Lord.
Celebrant	Let us give thanks to the Lord our God.
People	It is just and right so to do.

The Celebrant continues

It is right, and a good and joyful thing, always and everywhere to give thanks to you, Father Almighty, Creator of heaven and earth.

Here a Proper Preface is sung or said

Therefore we praise you, joining our voices with Angels and Archangels and with all the company of heaven, who forever sing this hymn to proclaim the glory of your Name:

The Sanctus

Celebrant and People

Holy, Holy, Holy, Lord God of power and might, heaven and earth are full of your glory.
  Hosanna in the highest.
Blessed is he who comes in the name of the Lord.
  Hosanna in the highest.

The Prayer of Consecration

The People stand or kneel. The Celebrant continues

All praise and glory is yours, God our heavenly Father, because of your tender mercy, you gave your only Son Jesus Christ to suffer death upon the cross for our redemption; who made there, by his one oblation of himself once offered, a full, perfect, and sufficient sacrifice, oblation, and satisfaction, for the sins of the whole world; and instituted, and in his Holy Gospel commanded us to continue a perpetual memory of his precious death and sacrifice, until his coming again.

And now, O merciful Father; in your great goodness, we ask you to bless and sanctify, with your Word and Holy Spirit, these gifts of bread and wine, that we, receiving them according to your Son our Savior Jesus Christ's holy institution, in remembrance of his death and passion, may be partakers of his most blessed Body and Blood.

At the following words concerning the bread, the Celebrant is to hold it, or lay a hand upon it, and here* may break the bread; and at the words concerning the cup, to hold or place a hand upon the cup and any other vessel containing the wine to be consecrated.

On the night that he was betrayed, our Lord Jesus Christ took bread; and when he had given thanks, he broke it,* and gave it to his disciples, saying, "Take, eat; this is my Body which is given for you: Do this in remembrance of me."

Likewise, after supper, Jesus took the cup, and when he had given thanks, he gave it to them, saying, "Drink this, all of you; for this is my Blood of the New Covenant, which is shed for you, and for many, for the forgiveness of sins: Whenever you drink it, do this in remembrance of me."

And therefore, O Lord and heavenly Father, according to the institution of your dearly beloved Son our Savior Jesus Christ, we your humble servants celebrate and make here before your divine Majesty, with these holy gifts, which we now offer you, the memorial which your Son commanded us to make; remembering his blessed passion and precious death, his mighty resurrection and glorious ascension and his promise to come again: and offering our wholehearted thanks to you for the countless benefits given to us by the same.

And we earnestly desire your fatherly goodness mercifully to accept this our sacrifice of praise and thanksgiving; asking you to grant that by the merits and death of your Son Jesus Christ, and through faith in his Blood, we and all your whole Church may obtain forgiveness of our sins, and all other benefits of his passion.

And here we offer and present to you, O Lord, ourselves, our souls and bodies, to be a reasonable, holy, and living sacrifice; humbly pleading that all those who shall partake of this Holy Communion may worthily receive the most precious Body and Blood of your Son Jesus Christ; that, by the Holy Spirit, we may be filled with your grace and heavenly benediction, and made one body with him, so that he may dwell in us, and we in him.

And although we are unworthy, because of our many sins, to offer you any sacrifice, yet we pray that you will accept this, the duty and service we owe, not weighing our merits, but pardoning our offenses, through Jesus Christ our Lord.

By him, and with him, and in him, in the unity of the Holy Spirit, all honor and glory is yours, Almighty Father, now and forever. *Amen.*

The Lord's Prayer

The Celebrant then says

And now as our Savior Christ has taught us, we are bold to pray:

Celebrant and People together pray

Our Father, who art in heaven, hallowed be thy Name.
Thy kingdom come, thy will be done, on earth as it is in heaven.
Give us this day our daily bread. And forgive us our trespasses,
	as we forgive those who trespass against us.
And lead us not into temptation, but deliver us from evil.
For thine is the kingdom, and the power, and the glory
	forever and ever. Amen.

or this

Our Father in heaven, hallowed be your Name. Your kingdom come,
	your will be done, on earth as it is in heaven.
Give us today our daily bread.
And forgive us our sins as we forgive those who sin against us.
Save us from the time of trial, and deliver us from evil.
For the kingdom, the power, and the glory are yours
	now and forever. Amen.

The Fraction

The Celebrant breaks the consecrated Bread. A period of silence is kept.

Then may be sung or said

Celebrant	[Alleluia.] Christ our Passover is sacrificed for us
People	Therefore let us keep the feast. [Alleluia.]

or this

Celebrant	[Alleluia.] Christ our Passover Lamb has been sacrificed, once for all upon the cross.
People	Therefore let us keep the feast. [Alleluia.]

In Lent, Alleluia is omitted, and may be omitted at other times except during Easter season.

The Prayer of Humble Access

Celebrant and People together

We do not presume to come to this your table, merciful Lord,
trusting in our own righteousness,
but in your abundant and great mercies.
We are not worthy so much as to gather up the crumbs under your
   table.
But you are the same Lord, who always delights in showing mercy.
Grant us, therefore, gracious Lord,
so to eat the flesh of your dear Son Jesus Christ and to drink his
   blood,
that our sinful bodies may be made clean by his body,
and our souls washed through his most precious blood,
and that we may evermore dwell in him, and he in us. Amen.

The Agnus Dei

The following or some other suitable anthem may be sung or said here

Lamb of God, you take away the sin of the world,
   have mercy on us.
Lamb of God, you take away the sin of the world,
   have mercy on us.
Lamb of God, you take away the sin of the world,
   grant us your peace.

The Ministration of Communion

Facing the People, the Celebrant may say the following invitation

The gifts of God for the people of God. [Take them in remembrance
that Christ died for you and feed on him in your hearts by faith, with
thanksgiving.]

or this

Behold the Lamb of God, behold him who takes away the sins of the world. Blessed are those who are invited to the marriage supper of the Lamb.
John 1:29, Revelation 19:9

The Ministers receive the Sacrament in both kinds, and then immediately deliver it to the People.

The Bread and Cup are given to the communicants with these words

The body of our Lord Jesus Christ, which was given for you, preserve your body and soul to everlasting life. [Take and eat this in remembrance that Christ died for you, and feed on him in your heart by faith, with thanksgiving.]

The blood of our Lord Jesus Christ, which was shed for you, preserve your body and soul to everlasting life. [Drink this in remembrance that Christ's blood was shed for you, and be thankful.]

During the ministration of Communion, hymns, psalms, or anthems may be sung.

The Celebrant may offer a sentence of Scripture at the conclusion of the Communion.

The Post Communion Prayer

After Communion, the Celebrant says

Let us pray.

Celebrant and People together

Almighty and ever-living God,
we thank you for feeding us, in these holy mysteries,
with the spiritual food of the most precious Body and Blood
of your Son our Savior Jesus Christ;
and for assuring us, through this Sacrament, of your favor and
    goodness towards us;
and that we are true members of the mystical body of your Son,
the blessed company of all faithful people;
and are also heirs, through hope, of your everlasting kingdom.
And we humbly ask you, heavenly Father,

to assist us with your grace,
that we may continue in that holy fellowship,
and do all such good works as you have prepared for us to walk in;
through Jesus Christ our Lord,
to whom with you and the Holy Spirit,
be all honor and glory, now and forever. Amen.

or this

Heavenly Father,
we thank you for feeding us with the spiritual food
of the most precious body and blood of your Son our Savior Jesus
    Christ:
and for assuring us in these holy mysteries
that we are living members of the body of your Son,
and heirs of your eternal Kingdom.
And now Father, send us out into the world to do the work you have
    given us to do,
to love and serve you as faithful witnesses of Christ our Lord.
To him, to you, and to the Holy Spirit,
be honor and glory, now and forever. Amen.

The Blessing

The Bishop when present, or the Priest, gives this or a seasonal blessing

The peace of God which passes all understanding keep your hearts
and minds in the knowledge and love of God, and of his Son Jesus
Christ our Lord; and the blessing of God Almighty, the Father, the
Son, and the Holy Spirit, be among you, and remain with you always.
Amen.

A hymn, psalm or anthem may be sung after the Blessing (or following the Dismissal).

The Dismissal

The Deacon, or the Priest, may dismiss the people with these words

	Let us go forth in the name of Christ.
People	Thanks be to God.

or this

Deacon	Go in peace to love and serve the Lord.
People	Thanks be to God.

or this

Deacon	Let us go forth into the world, rejoicing in the power of the Holy Spirit.
People	Thanks be to God.

or this

Deacon	Let us bless the Lord.
People	Thanks be to God.

From the Easter Vigil through the Day of Pentecost "Alleluia, alleluia" may be added to any of the dismissals.

The People respond

Thanks be to God. Alleluia, Alleluia.

Seasonal Greetings

The standard greeting may be replaced by a greeting appropriate to the season or the occasion, such as the following

For Advent

Celebrant	Surely the Lord is coming soon,
People	Amen. Come Lord Jesus!
	Revelation 22:20

From Christmas Eve until the Presentation of Christ

Celebrant	For unto us a child is born.
People	To us a son is given.
	Isaiah 9:6

From Ash Wednesday to the Eve of Palm Sunday or penitential occasions

Celebrant	Bless the Lord who forgives all our sins.
People	His mercy endures forever.

For Holy Week

Celebrant	Blessed be our God.
People	Now and forever. Amen.

From Easter Eve until the Eve of Pentecost

Celebrant	Alleluia! Christ is risen!
People	The Lord is risen indeed! Alleluia!

For the Day of Pentecost, and occasions of Confirmation and Ordination

Celebrant	The Lord will pour out his Spirit upon all flesh,
People	And your sons and daughters shall prophesy.
Celebrant	Your old men shall dream dreams,
People	and your young men shall see visions.
Celebrant	You shall know that the Lord is in the midst of Israel,
People	that he is the Lord and there is none else.

Celebrant	And it shall come to pass
People	that everyone who calls on the name of the Lord shall be saved.
	Joel 2:27-28, 32; Acts 2:17, 21

For All Saints' Day and other appropriate occasions

Celebrant	Worthy is the Lord our God
People	To receive glory and honor and power.
	Revelation 4:11

Proper Prefaces

Preface of the Lord's Day

Through Jesus Christ our Lord; who on the first day of the week overcame death and the grave, and by his glorious resurrection opened to us the way of everlasting life.

Advent

Because you sent your beloved Son to redeem us from sin and death, and to make us heirs in him of everlasting life; that when he shall come again in power and great glory to judge the world, we may without shame or fear rejoice to behold his appearing.

Christmas

Because you gave Jesus Christ, your only Son, to be born for us; who, by the working of the Holy Spirit, was made truly man, taking on the flesh of the Virgin Mary his mother; and yet without the stain of sin, to make us clean from sin.

Epiphany

Through Jesus Christ our Lord, who took on our mortal flesh to reveal His glory; that he might bring us out of darkness and into his own glorious light.

Presentation, Annunciation, and Transfiguration

Because in the mystery of the Word made flesh, you have caused a new light to shine in our hearts, to give the knowledge of your glory in the face of your Son Jesus Christ our Lord.

Lent

Because you have given us the spirit of discipline, that we may
triumph over the flesh, and live no longer for ourselves but for
Him who died for us and rose again, your Son Jesus Christ our Lord.

Holy Week

Because you gave your only Son, our Savior Jesus Christ, to redeem
mankind from the power of darkness; who, having finished the work
you gave him to do, was lifted high upon the cross that he might
draw the whole world to himself, and, being made perfect through
suffering, might become the author of eternal salvation to all who
obey him.

Maundy Thursday

Through Jesus Christ our Lord; who having loved his own who were
in the world, loved them to the end, and on the night before he
suffered, instituted these holy mysteries; that we, receiving the
benefits of his passion and resurrection, might be made partakers of
his divine nature.

Easter

But chiefly are we bound to praise you for the glorious resurrection
of your Son Jesus Christ our Lord: for he is the true Paschal Lamb,
which was offered for us, and has taken away the sin of the world;
who by his death has destroyed death, and by his rising to life again
has restored us to everlasting life.

Ascension

Through your most dearly beloved Son Jesus Christ our Lord; who
after his most glorious resurrection, appeared to his Apostles, and in
their sight ascended up into heaven, to prepare a place for us; that
where he is, there we might also ascend, and reign with him in glory.

Pentecost

Through Jesus Christ our Lord; according to whose most true promise, the Holy Spirit came down from heaven, lighting upon the disciples, to teach them, and to lead them into all truth; giving them boldness and fervent zeal constantly to preach the Gospel to all nations; by which we have been brought out of darkness and error into the clear light and true knowledge of you, and of your Son Jesus Christ.

Trinity Sunday

Who, with your co-eternal Son, and Holy Spirit, are one God, one Lord, in Trinity of Persons and in Unity of Substance. For that which we believe of your glory, O Father, we believe the same of your Son, and of the Holy Spirit, without any: difference of inequality.

All Saints

For in the multitude of your Saints, you have surrounded us with so great a cloud of witnesses that we, rejoicing in their fellowship, may run with patience the race that is set before us, and, together with them, may receive the crown of glory that does not fade away.

Apostles and Ordinations

Through the great shepherd of your flock, Jesus Christ our Lord; who after his resurrection sent forth his apostles to preach the Gospel and to teach all nations; and promised to be with them always, even to the end of the ages.

Dedication of a Church

Through Jesus Christ our great High Priest; in whom we are built up as living stones of a holy temple, that we might offer before you a sacrifice of praise and prayer which is holy and pleasing in your sight.

Baptism

Because in Jesus Christ our Lord, you have received us as your sons and daughters, made us citizens of your kingdom, and given us the Holy Spirit to guide us into all truth.

Marriage

Because in the love of wife and husband, you have given us an image of the heavenly Jerusalem, adorned as a bride for her bridegroom, your Son Jesus Christ our Lord; who loves her and gave himself for her, that he might make the whole creation new.

Offertory Sentences

Remember the words of the Lord Jesus, how he himself said "It is more blessed to give than to receive."
Acts 20:35

Let your light so shine before others, so that they may see your good works and give glory to your Father who is in heaven.
Matthew 5:16

Do not lay up for yourselves treasures on earth, where moth and rust destroy and where thieves break in and steal, but lay up for yourselves treasures in heaven, where neither moth nor rust destroys and where thieves do not break in and steal. For where your treasure is, there your heart will be also.
Matthew 6:19-21

Not everyone who says to me, "Lord, Lord," will enter the kingdom of heaven, but the one who does the will of my Father who is in heaven.
Matthew 7:21

Whoever sows sparingly will also reap sparingly, and whoever sows bountifully will also reap bountifully. Each one must give as he has decided in his heart, not reluctantly or under compulsion, for God loves a cheerful giver.
2 Corinthians 9:6-7

As we have opportunity, let us do good to everyone, and especially to those who are of the household of faith.
Galatians 6:10

For God is not unjust so as to overlook your work and the love that you have shown for his name in serving the saints, as you still do.
Hebrews 6:10

Do not neglect to do good and to share what you have, for such sacrifices are pleasing to God.
Hebrews 13:16

If anyone has the world's goods and sees his brother in need, yet closes his heart against him, how does God's love abide in him?
1 John 3:17

If you have many possessions, make your gift from them in proportion; if few, do not be afraid to give according to the little you have. So you will be laying up a good treasure for yourself against the day of necessity.
Tobit 4:8-9

And the King will answer them, "Truly, I say to you, as you did it to one of the least of these my brothers, you did it to me."
Matthew 25:40

How then will they call on him in whom they have not believed? And how are they to believe in him of whom they have never heard? And how are they to hear without someone preaching? And how are they to preach unless they are sent?
Romans 10:14-15

And Jesus said to them, "The harvest is plentiful, but the laborers are few. Therefore pray earnestly to the Lord of the harvest to send out laborers into his harvest."
Luke 10:2

They shall not appear before the Lord empty-handed. Every man shall give as he is able, according to the blessing of the Lord your God that he has given you.
Deuteronomy 16:16-17

Offer to God a sacrifice of thanksgiving, and perform your vows to the Most High.
Psalm 50:14

Ascribe to the Lord the glory due his name; bring an offering, and come into his courts!
Psalm 96:8

Walk in love, as Christ loved us and gave himself up for us, a fragrant offering and sacrifice to God.
Ephesians 5:2

I appeal to you therefore, brothers [and sisters], by the mercies of God, to present your bodies as a living sacrifice, holy and acceptable to God, which is your spiritual worship.
Romans 12:1

For you know the grace of our Lord Jesus Christ, that though he was rich, yet for your sake he became poor, so that you by his poverty might become rich.
2 Corinthians 8:9

You are a chosen race, a royal priesthood, a holy nation, a people for his own possession, that you may proclaim the excellencies of him who called you out of darkness into his marvelous light.
1 Peter 2:9

The Exhortation

Dearly beloved in the Lord: if you intend to come to the Holy Communion of the Body and Blood of our Savior Jesus Christ, you must consider how Saint Paul, in his Letter to the Corinthians, exhorts us all diligently to examine ourselves before we presume to eat of that Bread, and drink of that Cup. For as the benefit is great, if we receive that holy Sacrament with a truly penitent heart and lively faith; spiritually eating the flesh of Christ and drinking his blood, so that we might be made one with Christ and he with us; so also is the danger great, if we receive the same unworthily. For then we become guilty of profaning the Body and Blood of Christ our Savior, and we eat and drink to our own condemnation.

Therefore, judge yourself lest you be judged by the Lord. First, examine your life by the rule of God's commandments. Wherever you have offended, either by thought, word, or deed, there confess your sins to Almighty God, with the full intention to amend your life; be ready to make restitution for all injuries and wrongs done by you to others; and also be ready to forgive others who have offended you: for otherwise, if you unworthily receive Holy Communion, you will increase your own condemnation. Therefore, repent of your sins, or else do not come to God's Holy Table.

If you have come here today with a troubled conscience, and you need help and counsel, come to me, or to some other priest, and confess your sins; that you may receive godly counsel, direction, and absolution. To do so will both satisfy your conscience and remove any scruples or doubt.

Above all, each of us should give humble and hearty thanks to God, for the redemption of the world by the death and passion of our Savior Jesus Christ. He humbled himself, even to death on a cross, for us sinners who lay in darkness and in the shadow of death; that he might make us children of God, and exalt us to everlasting life.

Because of his exceedingly great love for us, our Savior Jesus Christ has instituted and ordained these holy mysteries as pledges of his love, and for a continual remembrance of his death and passion, to our great and endless comfort.

To him, therefore, with the Father and the Holy Spirit, let us give continual thanks, as is our duty and our joy; submitting ourselves entirely to his holy will and striving to serve him in holiness and righteousness all the days of our life. *Amen.*

The Decalogue

Exodus *20:1-17; Deuteronomy 5:6-21*

Celebrant   God spoke these words and said: I am the Lord your
              God, you shall have no other gods but me.
People   Lord, have mercy upon us, and give us grace to keep
              this law.

Celebrant   You shall not make for yourself any image or likeness of
              anything that is in heaven above, or in the earth beneath,
              or in the waters under the earth; you shall not bow down
              to them or worship them.
People   Lord, have mercy upon us, and give us grace to keep
              this law.

Celebrant   You shall not take the name of the Lord your God
              in vain.
People   Lord, have mercy upon us, and give us grace to keep
              this law.

Celebrant   Remember the Sabbath day and keep it holy.
People   Lord, have mercy upon us, and give us grace to keep
              this law.

Celebrant   Honor your father and your mother.
People   Lord, have mercy upon us, and give us grace to keep
              this law.

Celebrant   You shall not murder.
People   Lord, have mercy upon us, and give us grace to keep
              this law.

Celebrant	You shall not commit adultery.
People	Lord, have mercy upon us, and give us grace to keep this law.
Celebrant	You shall not steal.
People	Lord, have mercy upon us, and give us grace to keep this law.
Celebrant	You shall not bear false witness against your neighbor.
People	Lord, have mercy upon us, and give us grace to keep this law.
Celebrant	You shall not covet.
People	Lord, have mercy upon us, give us grace to keep these laws, and write them upon our hearts.

General Instructions

Before the celebration of Holy Communion, the Holy Table should be covered with a clean white cloth. As the oblations are placed upon the Holy Table by the Deacon or Celebrant, it is customary to add a little water to the wine.

If any consecrated Bread or Wine remains after the Communion, it may be reserved for future reception in a safe place set aside for that purpose. Apart from that which is to be reserved, the Priest or Deacon, and other communicants, shall reverently consume the remaining consecrated Bread and Wine either after the Ministration of Communion or after the Dismissal.

In the absence of a Priest, the Bishop may, at his discretion, authorize a Deacon to distribute Holy Communion to the congregation from consecrated Bread and Wine. In this situation, the Deacon may say all that is appointed through the Offertory, though the Deacon may not pronounce an absolution after the Confession. After the Offertory, the Deacon shall reverently place the consecrated Sacrament on the Holy Table. The Deacon then leads the people in the Lord's Prayer. Omitting the breaking of the bread, the Deacon proceeds with the rest of the liturgy. There is no blessing at the end of the liturgy.

When the Priest is assisted by a Deacon or another Priest, it is customary for the presiding Priest to administer the consecrated Bread. The administration of consecrated Bread and Wine by Priests, Deacons and authorized laity shall be determined by the Ordinary.

If the consecrated Bread or Wine does not suffice for the number of communicants, the Celebrant shall return to the Holy Table and consecrate more of either or both using the prayer of consecration; beginning with "And now, O merciful Father, in your great goodness" (Long Form) or "So now, Father, we ask you to bless and sanctify" (Short Form) and ending with the appropriate words of institution for either the Bread or the Wine or both.

Where the greeting "The Lord be with you" is used, the response "And also with you" may be used in place of "And with your spirit."

A Penitential Order, for use at the opening of the liturgy, or for use on other occasions, may be developed from among these texts provided within the Holy

Communion rite: Acclamation, Decalogue, Summary of the Law, Kyrie, Confession and Absolution, and the Comfortable Words.

Concerning Discipline

If the Priest knows that a person who is living a notoriously evil life intends to come to Communion, the Priest shall speak to that person privately, and tell him/her that he/she may not come to the Lord's Table until he/she has given clear proof of repentance and amendment of life. The Priest shall follow the same procedure with those who have done wrong to their neighbors and are a scandal to the other members of the congregation, not allowing such persons to receive Communion until they have made restitution for the wrong they have done.

When the Priest sees that there is enmity between members of the congregation, he/she shall speak privately to each of them, telling them that they may not receive Communion until they have forgiven each other. And if the person or persons on one side truly forgive the others and desire and promise to make up for their faults, but those on the other side refuse to forgive, the Priest shall allow those who are penitent to come to Communion, but not those who are obstinate.

In all such cases, the Priest is required to notify the Bishop, within fourteen days at the most, giving the reasons for refusing Communion. This is intended to give sufficient time for the repentance and reconciliation of the parties so involved.

College of Bishops Resolution Concerning the Nicene Creed (Epiphany, 2013, adopted unanimously)

Resolved,

The normative form of the Nicene Creed for the Anglican Church in North America is the original text as adopted by the Councils of Nicaea (325 A.D.) and Constantinople (381 A.D.). This form shall be rendered in English in the best and most accurate translation achievable.

Resolved,

The Anglican Church in North America acknowledges that the form of the Nicene Creed customary in the West is that of the 1662 Book of Common Prayer, including the words "and the Son" (filioque), which form may be used in worship and for elucidation of doctrine.

Resolved,

Because we are committed to the highest level of global unity possible, the College of Bishops of the Anglican Church in North America seeks advice of the Theological Commission of the Global Fellowship of Confessing Anglicans concerning implementation of the recommendation of the Lambeth Conference of 1978 to use the normative form of the Nicene Creed at worship.

The Order for the Administration of

the Lord's Supper

or

Holy Communion,

commonly called

The Holy Eucharist

Short Form

Approved for Provincial Use

The Anglican Church in North America

Petertide, A.D. 2013

A hymn, psalm, or anthem may be sung.

The Acclamation

The People standing, the Celebrant says this or a seasonal greeting as found on pages 94-95

Blessed be God, the Father, the Son, and the Holy Spirit.
People   And blessed be his kingdom, now and forever. Amen.

In place of the above, from Easter Day through the Day of Pentecost

Celebrant   Alleluia. Christ is risen.
People   The Lord is risen indeed. Alleluia.

The Collect for Purity

The Celebrant prays (and the People may be invited to join)

Almighty God, to you all hearts are open, all desires known, and from you no secrets are hid: Cleanse the thoughts of our hearts by the inspiration of your Holy Spirit, that we may perfectly love you, and worthily magnify your holy Name; through Christ our Lord. Amen.

The Summary of the Law

The Celebrant then reads the Summary of the Law. The Decalogue may be used at any time in place of the Summary of the Law. It is appropriate to use the Decalogue throughout the seasons of Advent and Lent and on other penitential occasions.

Jesus said: You shall love the Lord your God with all your heart and with all your soul and with all your mind. This is the great and first commandment. And a second is like it: You shall love your neighbor as yourself. On these two commandments depend all the Law and the Prophets.
Matthew 22:37-40

Kyrie

The Celebrant and People may sing or pray together once or three times

Lord, have mercy [upon us].	*or*	Kyrie eleison.
Christ, have mercy [upon us].		*Christe eleison.*
Lord, have mercy [upon us].		Kyrie eleison.

or this

Trisagion

Holy God,
Holy and Mighty,
Holy Immortal One,
Have mercy upon us.

Gloria in Excelsis

The Gloria or some other song of praise may be sung or said, all standing. It is appropriate to omit the song of praise during penitential seasons and days appointed for fasting. The Gloria may alternatively be placed immediately before the Blessing and Dismissal.

Glory to God in the highest,
   and peace to his people on earth.
Lord God, heavenly King,
almighty God and Father,
   we worship you, we give you thanks,
   we praise you for your glory.
Lord Jesus Christ, only Son of the Father,
Lord God, Lamb of God,
you take away the sin of the world:
   have mercy on us;
you are seated at the right hand of the Father:
   receive our prayer.
For you alone are the Holy One,
you alone are the Lord,
you alone are the Most High,
   Jesus Christ,
   with the Holy Spirit,
   in the glory of God the Father. Amen.

The Collect of the Day

The Celebrant says to the People

	The Lord be with you.
People	And with your spirit.
Celebrant	Let us pray.

The Celebrant prays the Collect. When concluded, the people respond praying

People	Amen.

The Lessons

One or more Lessons, as appointed, are read, the Reader first saying

A Reading from _____.

A citation giving chapter and verse may be added.

After each Lesson, the Reader may say

The Word of the Lord.
People   Thanks be to God.

Silence may follow.

A psalm, hymn or anthem may follow each reading.

All standing, the Deacon or Priest reads the Gospel, first saying

The Holy Gospel of our Lord Jesus Christ according
to _____.
People   Glory to you, Lord Christ.

After the Gospel, the Reader says

The Gospel of the Lord.
People   Praise to you, Lord Christ.

The Sermon

Nicene Creed

*On Sundays, other Major Feast Days, and other times as appointed, all stand to recite the
Nicene Creed, the Celebrant first saying*

Let us confess our faith in the words of the Nicene Creed:

Celebrant and People

We believe in one God,
    the Father, the Almighty,
    maker of heaven and earth,
    of all that is, visible and invisible.

We believe in one Lord, Jesus Christ,
   the only Son of God,
   eternally begotten of the Father,
   God from God, Light from Light,
   true God from true God,
   begotten, not made,
   of one Being with the Father;
   through him all things were made.
   For us and for our salvation he came down from heaven,
   was incarnate from the Holy Spirit and the Virgin Mary,
   and was made man.
   For our sake he was crucified under Pontius Pilate;
   he suffered death and was buried.
   On the third day he rose again in accordance with the Scriptures;
   he ascended into heaven
   and is seated at the right hand of the Father.
   He will come again in glory to judge the living and the dead,
   and his kingdom will have no end.

We believe in the Holy Spirit, the Lord, the giver of life,
   who proceeds from the Father [and the Son]*,
   who with the Father and the Son is worshiped and glorified,
   who has spoken through the prophets.
   We believe in one holy catholic and apostolic Church.
   We acknowledge one baptism for the forgiveness of sins.
   We look for the resurrection of the dead,
   and the life of the world to come. Amen.

---

* The *filioque* [and the Son] is not in the original Greek text. Nevertheless, in the
Western Church the *filioque* [and the Son] is customary at worship and is used for
the explication of doctrine [*39 Articles of Religion*]. The operative resolution of the
College of Bishops concerning use of the *filioque* is printed with the General
Instructions at the end of the Holy Communion, Long Form.

The Prayers of the People

The Prayers, the Exhortation, the Confession and Absolution and the Peace may alternatively be placed after the Offertory. After each petition there may be a time of silence for the Clergy and People to add their own prayers.

The Deacon or other person appointed may say

Let us pray for the whole state of Christ's Church and the world.

Almighty and ever-living God, in your holy Word you have taught us to offer prayers and requests, and to give thanks for all whom you have made. We appeal to your mercy, Gracious Lord, that you might hear our prayer.

Reader Lord, in your mercy,
People hear our prayer.

Inspire your universal Church by your Spirit, granting that all who confess your holy Name may agree in the truth of your holy Word and live in unity and godly love.

Reader Lord, in your mercy,
People hear our prayer.

Give grace, heavenly Father, to all Bishops, Priests, and Deacons, *and especially to your servant(s) N, our Archbishop/Bishop/Priest/Deacon etc.*, that by their life and teaching, they may proclaim your true and life-giving Word, and rightly administer your holy Sacraments.

Reader Lord, in your mercy,
People hear our prayer.

Help us to fulfill your great commission; making disciples of all nations; teaching them to obey all that you have commanded.

Reader Lord, in your mercy,
People hear our prayer.

We ask you to rule the hearts of all who govern us, especially *N*, our *President/Prime Minister/Sovereign.* May they administer justice, govern wisely, and strive for the welfare and peace of the whole world.

Reader	Lord, in your mercy,
People	hear our prayer.

Grant your heavenly grace to all people, especially these gathered here, that with meek and reverent hearts, we may hear and trust your holy Word, devoting our lives to your righteous service.

Reader	Lord, in your mercy,
People	hear our prayer.

We humbly ask you, gracious Lord, to comfort and strengthen all those who, in this earthly life are in trouble, sorrow, need, sickness, or any other adversity.

Reader	Lord, in your mercy,
People	hear our prayer.

Reader	I invite you to add your own requests at this time.

We bless your holy Name for all your servants who departed this life in your faith and fear, praying you would grant us grace to follow their good examples, that with them we might partake in your heavenly kingdom.

Reader	Lord, in your mercy,
People	hear our prayer.

The Celebrant concludes with the following prayer

Grant these our prayers, O Father, for Jesus Christ's sake, our only Mediator and Advocate. *Amen.*

The Exhortation

It is customary for the Celebrant to say the Exhortation on the First Sunday in Advent, the First Sunday in Lent, and on Trinity Sunday.

The Confession and Absolution of Sin

The Deacon or other person appointed says the following

We pray to you also for the forgiveness of our sins.

The Deacon and People kneel as able and pray

Most merciful God,
we confess that we have sinned against you
in thought, word and deed,
by what we have done, and by what we have left undone.
We have not loved you with our whole heart;
we have not loved our neighbors as ourselves.
We are truly sorry and we humbly repent.
For the sake of your Son Jesus Christ,
have mercy on us and forgive us;
that we may delight in your will, and walk in your ways,
to the glory of your Name. Amen.

The Bishop or Priest stands and says

Almighty God, our heavenly Father, who in his great mercy has
promised forgiveness of sins to all those who sincerely repent and with
true faith turn to him, have mercy upon you, pardon and deliver you
from all your sins, confirm and strengthen you in all goodness, and
bring you to everlasting life; through Jesus Christ our Lord. *Amen.*

The Peace

Celebrant   The Peace of the Lord be always with you.
People   And with your spirit.

Then the Ministers and People may greet one another in the name of the Lord.

The Offertory

The Celebrant may begin the Offertory with one of the provided sentences of Scripture.

*During the Offertory a hymn, psalm, or anthem may be sung. The Deacon or Priest prepares
the Holy Table for the celebration. Representatives of the congregation bring the People's
offerings of bread and wine, and money or other gifts, to the Deacon or Priest.*

The People stand while the offerings are presented.

Yours, O Lord, is the greatness, and the power, and the glory, and the victory, and the majesty: for everything in heaven and on earth is yours; yours is the kingdom, O Lord, and you are exalted as Head above all. All things come from you, O Lord, and of your own have we given you.
1 Chronicles 29:11, 14

The Sursum Corda

The People remain standing. The Celebrant faces them and sings or says

	The Lord be with you.
People	And with your spirit.
Celebrant	Lift up your hearts.
People	We lift them to the Lord.
Celebrant	Let us give thanks to the Lord our God.
People	It is just and right so to do.

Celebrant

It is right, and a good and joyful thing, always and everywhere to give thanks to you, Father Almighty, Creator of heaven and earth.

Here a Proper Preface is sung or said

Therefore we praise you, joining our voices with Angels and Archangels and with all the company of heaven, who forever sing this hymn to proclaim the glory of your Name:

The Sanctus

Celebrant and People

Holy, Holy, Holy, Lord God of power and might,
heaven and earth are full of your glory.
　　Hosanna in the highest.
Blessed is he who comes in the name of the Lord.
　　Hosanna in the highest.

The Prayer of Consecration

The People stand or kneel. The Celebrant continues

Almighty God, our heavenly Father, in your tender mercy, you gave your only Son Jesus Christ to suffer death upon the cross for our redemption. He offered himself and made, once for all time, a perfect and sufficient sacrifice for the sins of the whole world. He instituted this remembrance of his passion and death, which he commanded us to continue until he comes again. So now, Father, we ask you to bless and sanctify, with your Word and Holy Spirit, these gifts of bread and wine that we may partake of his most blessed Body and Blood.

At the following words concerning the bread, the Celebrant is to hold it, or lay a hand upon it, and here* may break the bread; and at the words concerning the cup, to hold or place a hand upon the cup and any other vessel containing the wine to be consecrated.

On the night that he was betrayed, our Lord Jesus Christ took bread; and when he had given thanks, he broke it,* and gave it to his disciples, saying, "Take, eat; this is my Body which is given for you: Do this in remembrance of me."

After supper, Jesus took the cup, and when he had given thanks, he gave it to them, saying, "Drink this, all of you; for this is my Blood of the New Covenant, which is shed for you, and for many, for the forgiveness of sins: Whenever you drink it, do this in remembrance of me."

Therefore we proclaim the mystery of faith:

Celebrant and People

Christ has died.
Christ is risen.
Christ will come again.

The Celebrant continues

Lord and heavenly Father, with these holy gifts we celebrate the memorial instituted by your beloved Son, remembering his passion and death, his resurrection and ascension, and his promise to come again. Grant that by his merits and death, and through faith in his Blood, we and your whole Church may receive forgiveness of our sins and all other benefits of his passion, making us one body with him that he may dwell in us, and we in him. And here we offer to you, O Lord, ourselves, our souls and bodies, to be a living sacrifice, through Jesus Christ our Lord.

By him and with him and in him, in the unity of the Holy Spirit, all honor and glory is yours, Almighty Father, now and forever. *Amen.*

The Lord's Prayer

The Celebrant then says

And now as our Savior Christ has taught us, we are bold to pray

Celebrant and People together pray

Our Father, who art in heaven, hallowed be thy Name.
Thy kingdom come, thy will be done, on earth as it is in heaven.
Give us this day our daily bread.
And forgive us our trespasses, as we forgive those who trespass
    against us.
And lead us not into temptation, but deliver us from evil.
For thine is the kingdom, and the power, and the glory,
    forever and ever. Amen.

or this

Our Father in heaven, hallowed be your Name.
Your kingdom come, your will be done, on earth as it is in heaven.
Give us today our daily bread.
And forgive us our sins as we forgive those who sin against us.
Save us from the time of trial, and deliver us from evil.
For the kingdom, the power, and the glory are yours,
    now and forever. Amen.

The Fraction

The Celebrant breaks the consecrated Bread.

A period of silence is kept.

Then may be sung or said

Celebrant	[Alleluia.] Christ our Passover is sacrificed for us.
People	Therefore let us keep the feast. [Alleluia.]

or this

Celebrant	[Alleluia.] Christ our Passover Lamb has been sacrificed, once for all upon the cross.
People	Therefore let us keep the feast. [Alleluia.]

In Lent, Alleluia is omitted, and may be omitted at other times except during Easter season.

The Prayer of Humble Access

Celebrant and People together

We do not presume to come to this your table, merciful Lord,
trusting in our own righteousness,
but in your abundant and great mercies.
We are not worthy so much as to gather up the crumbs under your
    table.
But you are the same Lord, who always delights in showing mercy.
Grant us, therefore, gracious Lord,
so to eat the flesh of your dear Son Jesus Christ and to drink his
    blood,
that our sinful bodies may be made clean by his body,
and our souls washed through his most precious blood,
and that we may evermore dwell in him, and he in us. Amen.

The Agnus Dei

The following or some other suitable anthem may be sung or said here.

Lamb of God, you take away the sin of the world,
  have mercy on us.
Lamb of God, you take away the sin of the world,
  have mercy on us.
Lamb of God, you take away the sin of the world,
  grant us your peace.

The Ministration of Communion

Facing the People, the Celebrant may say the following invitation

The gifts of God for the People of God. [Take them in remembrance that Christ died for you and feed on him in your hearts by faith, with thanksgiving.]

or this

Behold the Lamb of God, behold him who takes away the sins of the world. Blessed are those who are invited to the marriage supper of the Lamb.
John 1:29, Revelation 19:9

The Ministers receive the Sacrament in both kinds, and then immediately deliver it to the People.

The Bread and Cup are given to the communicants with these words

The body of our Lord Jesus Christ, which was given for you, preserve your body and soul to everlasting life. [Take and eat this in remembrance that Christ died for you, and feed on him in your heart by faith, with thanksgiving.]

The blood of our Lord Jesus Christ, which was shed for you, preserve your body and soul to everlasting life. [Drink this in remembrance that Christ's blood was shed for you, and be thankful.]

During the ministration of Communion, hymns, psalms, or anthems may be sung.

The Celebrant may offer a sentence of Scripture at the conclusion of the Communion.

The Post Communion Prayer

After Communion, the Celebrant says

Let us pray.

Celebrant and People

Heavenly Father,
we thank you for feeding us with the spiritual food
of the most precious Body and Blood of your Son our Savior Jesus
    Christ;
and for assuring us in these holy mysteries
that we are living members of the Body of your Son,
and heirs of your eternal kingdom.
And now, Father, send us out into the world to do the work you have
    given us to do,
to love and serve you as faithful witnesses of Christ our Lord.
To him, to you, and to the Holy Spirit,
be honor and glory, now and forever. Amen.

The Blessing

The Bishop when present, or the Priest, gives this or a seasonal blessing

The peace of God which passes all understanding keep your hearts
and minds in the knowledge and love of God, and of his Son Jesus
Christ our Lord; and the blessing of God Almighty, the Father, the
Son, and the Holy Spirit, be among you, and remain with you always.
Amen.

A hymn, psalm or anthem may be sung after the Blessing (or following the Dismissal).

The Dismissal

The Deacon, or the Priest, may dismiss the people with these words

	Let us go forth in the name of Christ.
People	Thanks be to God.

or this

Deacon	Go in peace to love and serve the Lord.
People	Thanks be to God.

or this

Deacon	Let us go forth into the world, rejoicing in the power of the Holy Spirit.
People	Thanks be to God.

or this

Deacon	Let us bless the Lord.
People	Thanks be to God.

From the Easter Vigil through the Day of Pentecost "Alleluia, alleluia" may be added to any of the dismissals.

The People respond

Thanks be to God. Alleluia, Alleluia.

Seasonal Greetings

The standard greeting may be replaced by a greeting appropriate to the season or the occasion, such as the following

For Advent

Celebrant	Surely the Lord is coming soon,
People	Amen. Come Lord Jesus!
	Revelation 22:20

From Christmas Eve until the Presentation of Christ

Celebrant	For unto us a child is born.
People	To us a son is given.
	Isaiah 9:6

From Ash Wednesday to the Eve of Palm Sunday or penitential occasions

Celebrant	Bless the Lord who forgives all our sins.
People	His mercy endures forever.

For Holy Week

Celebrant	Blessed be our God.
People	Now and forever. Amen.

From Easter Eve until the Eve of Pentecost

Celebrant	Alleluia! Christ is risen!
People	The Lord is risen indeed! Alleluia!

For the Day of Pentecost, and occasions of Confirmation and Ordination

Celebrant	The Lord will pour out his Spirit upon all flesh,
People	And your sons and daughters shall prophesy.
Celebrant	Your old men shall dream dreams,
People	and your young men shall see visions.

Celebrant	You shall know that the Lord is in the midst of Israel,
People	that he is the Lord and there is none else.
Celebrant	And it shall come to pass
People	that everyone who calls on the name of the Lord shall be saved.
	Joel 2:27-28, 32; Acts 2:17, 21

For All Saints' Day and other appropriate occasions

Celebrant	Worthy is the Lord our God
People	To receive glory and honor and power.
	Revelation 4:11

Proper Prefaces

Preface of the Lord's Day

Through Jesus Christ our Lord; who on the first day of the week overcame death and the grave, and by his glorious resurrection opened to us the way of everlasting life.

Advent

Because you sent your beloved Son to redeem us from sin and death, and to make us heirs in him of everlasting life; that when he shall come again in power and great glory to judge the world, we may without shame or fear rejoice to behold his appearing.

Christmas

Because you gave Jesus Christ, your only Son, to be born for us; who, by the working of the Holy Spirit, was made truly man, taking on the flesh of the Virgin Mary his mother; and yet without the stain of sin, to make us clean from sin.

Epiphany

Through Jesus Christ our Lord, who took on our mortal flesh to reveal His glory; that he might bring us out of darkness and into his own glorious light.

Presentation, Annunciation, and Transfiguration

Because in the mystery of the Word made flesh, you have caused a new light to shine in our hearts, to give the knowledge of your glory in the face of your Son Jesus Christ our Lord.

Lent

Because you have given us the spirit of discipline, that we may triumph over the flesh, and live no longer for ourselves but for him who died for us and rose again, your Son Jesus Christ our Lord.

Holy Week

Because you gave your only Son, our Savior Jesus Christ, to redeem mankind from the power of darkness; who, having finished the work you gave him to do, was lifted high upon the cross that he might draw the whole world to himself, and, being made perfect through suffering, might become the author of eternal salvation to all who obey him.

Maundy Thursday

Through Jesus Christ our Lord; who having loved his own who were in the world, loved them to the end, and on the night before he suffered, instituted these holy mysteries; that we, receiving the benefits of his passion and resurrection, might be made partakers of his divine nature.

Easter

But chiefly are we bound to praise you for the glorious resurrection of your Son Jesus Christ our Lord: for he is the true Paschal Lamb, which was offered for us, and has taken away the sin of the world; who by his death has destroyed death, and by his rising to life again has restored us to everlasting life.

Ascension

Through your most dearly beloved Son Jesus Christ our Lord; who after his most glorious resurrection, appeared to his Apostles, and in their sight ascended up into heaven, to prepare a place for us; that where he is, there we might also ascend, and reign with him in glory.

Pentecost

Through Jesus Christ our Lord; according to whose most true promise, the Holy Spirit came down from heaven, lighting upon the disciples, to teach them, and to lead them into all truth; giving them boldness and fervent zeal constantly to preach the Gospel to all nations; by which we have been brought out of darkness and error into the clear light and true knowledge of you, and of your Son Jesus Christ.

Trinity Sunday

Who, with your co-eternal Son, and Holy Spirit, are one God, one Lord, in Trinity of Persons and in Unity of Substance. For that which we believe of your glory, O Father, we believe the same of your Son, and of the Holy Spirit, without any difference of inequality.

All Saints

For in the multitude of your Saints, you have surrounded us with so great a cloud of witnesses that we, rejoicing in their fellowship, may run with patience the race that is set before us, and, together with them, may receive the crown of glory that does not fade away.

Apostles and Ordinations

Through the great shepherd of your flock, Jesus Christ our Lord; who after his resurrection sent forth his apostles to preach the Gospel and to teach all nations; and promised to be with them always, even to the end of the ages.

Dedication of a Church

Through Jesus Christ our great High Priest; in whom we are built up as living stones of a holy temple, that we might offer before you a sacrifice of praise and prayer which is holy and pleasing in your sight.

Baptism

Because in Jesus Christ our Lord, you have received us as your sons and daughters, made us citizens of your kingdom, and given us the Holy Spirit to guide us into all truth.

Marriage

Because in the love of wife and husband, you have given us an image of the heavenly Jerusalem, adorned as a bride for her bridegroom, your Son Jesus Christ our Lord; who loves her and gave himself for her, that he might make the whole creation new.

Offertory Sentences

Remember the words of the Lord Jesus, how he himself said "It is more blessed to give than to receive."
Acts 20:35

Let your light so shine before others, so that they may see your good works and give glory to your Father who is in heaven.
Matthew 5:16

Do not lay up for yourselves treasures on earth, where moth and rust destroy and where thieves break in and steal, but lay up for yourselves treasures in heaven, where neither moth nor rust destroys and where thieves do not break in and steal. For where your treasure is, there your heart will be also.
Matthew 6:19-21

Not everyone who says to me, "Lord, Lord," will enter the kingdom of heaven, but the one who does the will of my Father who is in heaven.
Matthew 7:21

Whoever sows sparingly will also reap sparingly, and whoever sows bountifully will also reap bountifully. Each one must give as he has decided in his heart, not reluctantly or under compulsion, for God loves a cheerful giver.
2 Corinthians 9:6-7

As we have opportunity, let us do good to everyone, and especially to those who are of the household of faith.
Galatians 6:10

For God is not unjust so as to overlook your work and the love that you have shown for his name in serving the saints, as you still do.
Hebrews 6:10

Do not neglect to do good and to share what you have, for such sacrifices are pleasing to God.
Hebrews 13:16

If anyone has the world's goods and sees his brother in need, yet closes his heart against him, how does God's love abide in him?
1 John 3:17

If you have many possessions, make your gift from them in proportion; if few, do not be afraid to give according to the little you have. So you will be laying up a good treasure for yourself against the day of necessity.
Tobit 4:8-9

And the King will answer them, "Truly, I say to you, as you did it to one of the least of these my brothers, you did it to me."
Matthew 25:40

How then will they call on him in whom they have not believed? And how are they to believe in him of whom they have never heard? And how are they to hear without someone preaching? And how are they to preach unless they are sent?
Romans 10:14-15

And Jesus said to them, "The harvest is plentiful, but the laborers are few. Therefore pray earnestly to the Lord of the harvest to send out laborers into his harvest."
Luke 10:2

They shall not appear before the Lord empty-handed. Every man shall give as he is able, according to the blessing of the Lord your God that he has given you.
Deuteronomy 16:16-17

Offer to God a sacrifice of thanksgiving, and perform your vows to the Most High.
Psalm 50:14

Ascribe to the Lord the glory due his name; bring an offering, and come into his courts!
Psalm 96:8

Walk in love, as Christ loved us and gave himself up for us, a fragrant offering and sacrifice to God.
Ephesians 5:2

I appeal to you therefore, brothers [and sisters], by the mercies of God, to present your bodies as a living sacrifice, holy and acceptable to God, which is your spiritual worship.
Romans 12:1

For you know the grace of our Lord Jesus Christ, that though he was rich, yet for your sake he became poor, so that you by his poverty might become rich.
2 Corinthians 8:9

You are a chosen race, a royal priesthood, a holy nation, a people for his own possession, that you may proclaim the excellencies of him who called you out of darkness into his marvelous light.
1 Peter 2:9

The Exhortation

Dearly beloved in the Lord: if you intend to come to the Holy Communion of the Body and Blood of our Savior Jesus Christ, you must consider how Saint Paul, in his Letter to the Corinthians, exhorts us all diligently to examine ourselves before we presume to eat of that Bread, and drink of that Cup. For as the benefit is great, if we receive that holy Sacrament with a truly penitent heart and lively faith; spiritually eating the flesh of Christ and drinking his blood, so that we might be made one with Christ and he with us; so also is the danger great, if we receive the same unworthily. For then we become guilty of profaning the Body and Blood of Christ our Savior, and we eat and drink to our own condemnation.

Therefore, judge yourself lest you be judged by the Lord. First, examine your life by the rule of God's commandments. Wherever you have offended, either by thought, word, or deed, there confess your sins to Almighty God, with the full intention to amend your life; be ready to make restitution for all injuries and wrongs done by you to others; and also be ready to forgive others who have offended you: for otherwise, if you unworthily receive Holy Communion, you will increase your own condemnation. Therefore, repent of your sins, or else do not come to God's Holy Table.

If you have come here today with a troubled conscience, and you need help and counsel, come to me, or to some other priest, and confess your sins; that you may receive godly counsel, direction, and absolution. To do so will both satisfy your conscience and remove any scruples or doubt.

Above all, each of us should give humble and hearty thanks to God, for the redemption of the world by the death and passion of our Savior Jesus Christ. He humbled himself, even to death on a cross, for us sinners who lay in darkness and in the shadow of death; that he might make us children of God, and exalt us to everlasting life.

Because of his exceedingly great love for us, our Savior Jesus Christ has instituted and ordained these holy mysteries as pledges of his love, and for a continual remembrance of his death and passion, to our great and endless comfort.

To him, therefore, with the Father and the Holy Spirit, let us give continual thanks, as is our duty and our joy; submitting ourselves entirely to his holy will and striving to serve him in holiness and righteousness all the days of our life. *Amen.*

The Decalogue

Exodus *20:1-17; Deuteronomy 5:6-21*

Celebrant   God spoke these words and said: I am the Lord your God, you shall have no other gods but me.

People   Lord, have mercy upon us, and give us grace to keep this law.

Celebrant   You shall not make for yourself any image or likeness of anything that is in heaven above, or in the earth beneath, or in the waters under the earth; you shall not bow down to them or worship them.

People   Lord, have mercy upon us, and give us grace to keep this law.

Celebrant   You shall not take the name of the Lord your God in vain.

People   Lord, have mercy upon us, and give us grace to keep this law.

Celebrant   Remember the Sabbath day and keep it holy.

People   Lord, have mercy upon us, and give us grace to keep this law.

Celebrant   Honor your father and your mother.

People   Lord, have mercy upon us, and give us grace to keep this law.

Celebrant   You shall not murder.

People   Lord, have mercy upon us, and give us grace to keep this law.

Celebrant   You shall not commit adultery.

People   Lord, have mercy upon us, and give us grace to keep this law.

Celebrant	You shall not steal.
People	Lord, have mercy upon us, and give us grace to keep this law.
Celebrant	You shall not bear false witness against your neighbor.
People	Lord, have mercy upon us, and give us grace to keep this law.
Celebrant	You shall not covet.
People	Lord, have mercy upon us, give us grace to keep these laws, and write them upon our hearts.

General Instructions

The General Instructions concerning the celebration of Holy Communion are printed at the end of the Holy Communion, Long Form. These instructions apply equally to the Holy Communion, Short Form.

The Holy Communion, Long Form, is intended for use at the principal service(s) on the Lord's Day and for other major celebrations. The Holy Communion, Short Form, is intended for use at other times.

The Ordinal
of the
Anglican Church in North America

Being the Form and Manner of Ordaining Bishops, Priests, and Deacons

Authorized and Adopted

by the

College of Bishops

A.D. 2013

The Preface

It is clearly evident to anyone who diligently reads both the Holy Scriptures and ancient Authors, that from the Apostles' time these three Orders of ministry have existed in Christ's Church: Bishops, Priests, and Deacons. From the earliest days of the Church, these Offices were always held in such reverent estimation, that no one might presume to execute any of them, without being first called, tried, and examined, and ascertained to have such qualities as are requisite for the same. Candidates were approved and admitted thereunto by lawful Authority through public Prayer, and the Imposition of Hands. And therefore, to the intent that these Orders may be continued, and reverently used and esteemed in this Church, no one shall be accounted to be a lawful Bishop, Priest, or Deacon in this Church, or allowed to execute any of the said Functions, except they be called, tried, examined, and admitted thereunto, according to the Form set forth in this book, or have received Episcopal Consecration or Ordination already.

And none shall be admitted a Deacon, Priest, or Bishop, except they be of the age which the Canons may require.

And the Bishop, knowing either by himself, or by sufficient testimony, that a Person is of virtuous conduct, and without crime, after examination and trial, finding them sufficiently instructed in the Holy Scripture, and otherwise educated as the Canons require, may, in the presence of the Church, admit them as a Deacon, or admit a Deacon as a Priest, in such manner and form as follows.

The Form and Manner of Ordaining Deacons

A hymn, psalm, or anthem may be sung.

The People standing, the Bishop says this or an appropriate seasonal greeting

Blessed be God, the Father, the Son, and the Holy Spirit.

People   And blessed be his kingdom, now and forever. Amen.

In place of the above, from Easter Day through the Day of Pentecost

Bishop   Alleluia. Christ is risen.
People   The Lord is risen indeed. Alleluia.

In place of the above, on Ember days in the season of Lent

Bishop   Bless the Lord who forgives all our sins.
People   His mercy endures forever.

Bishop

Almighty God, to whom all hearts are open, all desires known, and from whom no secrets are hid: Cleanse the thoughts of our hearts by the inspiration of your Holy Spirit, that we may perfectly love you, and worthily magnify your holy Name; through Christ our Lord. Amen.

The Presentation

The Bishop and People sit. The Presenters, standing before the Bishop, shall present each Ordinand, saying

Right Reverend Father in God, we present *N.N.* to be admitted to the Order of Deacons.

Bishop   Have *these persons* been selected in accordance with the Canons of this Church? And do you believe *their* manner of life to be suitable to the exercise of this ministry?

| *Presenters* | We certify to you that *they* have satisfied the requirements of the Canons, and we believe *them* to be qualified for this order. |

The Bishop shall then require the Ordinands to take the Oath of Conformity saying

The Canons require that no one may be ordained a Deacon in the Church until such person has subscribed without reservation to the Oath of Conformity. It is also required that each Ordinand subscribe without reservation to the Oath of Canonical Obedience. In the presence of this congregation, I now charge you to make your solemn declaration of these oaths.

Each Ordinand then declares separately

I, *N.N.*, do believe the Holy Scriptures of the Old and New Testaments to be the Word of God and to contain all things necessary to salvation; and therefore I hold myself bound to conform my life and ministry thereto, and do solemnly engage to conform to the Doctrine, Discipline and Worship of Christ as this Church has received them.

Each Ordinand then declares the following Oath of Canonical Obedience as well, saying

And I do swear by Almighty God that I will pay true and canonical obedience in all things lawful and honest to the Bishop of _____, and his successors: So help me God.

Each Ordinand then signs the Oath of Conformity and the Oath of Canonical Obedience in the sight of all present.

All stand. The Bishop says to the People

Dear Brothers and Sisters in Christ, you know the importance of this ministry, and the weight of your responsibility in presenting *these persons* for ordination to the sacred Order of Deacons. Therefore if any of you know of any impediment or crime because of which we should not proceed, come forward now, and make it known.

If no objection is made, the Bishop continues

	Is it your will that *these persons* be ordained as Deacons?
People	It is.
Bishop	Will you uphold *them* in *their* ministry?
People	We will.
Bishop	In peace let us pray to the Lord.

The Litany for Ordinations

All kneel. Then the Bishop or Litanist appointed shall, with the Clergy and People present, say or sing the Litany for Ordinations. The Ordinands shall either kneel or lie prostrate during the Litany.

At the conclusion of the Litany for Ordinations, the Bishop shall stand and pray the following collect, first saying

	The Lord be with you.
People	And with your spirit.
Bishop	Let us pray.

Almighty God, who by your divine providence has appointed diverse Orders of Ministers in your Church, and who inspired your Apostles to choose into the Order of Deacons the first martyr Stephen, with others; mercifully behold *these* your *servants* now called to the same Office and Administration: so fill *them* with the truth of your Doctrine and adorn *them* with holiness of life, that, both by word and good example, *they* may faithfully serve you in this Office, to the glory of your Name and the edification of your Church; through the merits of our Savior Jesus Christ, your Son, our Lord, who lives and reigns with you and the Holy Spirit, world without end. *Amen.*

The Lessons

Following are the readings appointed for the ordination of a Deacon. On a Major Feast, or on a Sunday, the Bishop may select readings from the Proper of the Day.

Jeremiah 1:4-10
Psalm 119:1-8
1 Timothy 3:8-13 *or* Acts 6:1-7
Luke 12:35-40

The People sit. One or two Lessons, as appointed, are read, the Reader first saying

A Reading from _____.

A citation giving chapter and verse may be added.

After each Reading, the Reader shall say

The Word of the Lord.
People   Thanks be to God.

Silence may follow. A psalm, hymn, or anthem may follow each Reading.

The Gospel

Then, all standing, the Deacon or other Minister reads the Gospel, first saying

The Holy Gospel of our Lord Jesus Christ according to
        Saint _____.
People   Glory to you, Lord Christ.

After the Gospel, the Reader says

The Gospel of the Lord.
People   Praise to you, Lord Christ

The Sermon

The Nicene Creed

All stand to recite the Nicene Creed, the Bishop first saying

Let us confess our faith in the words of the Nicene Creed:

Bishop and People

We believe in one God,
        the Father, the Almighty,
        maker of heaven and earth,
        of all that is, visible and invisible.

We believe in one Lord, Jesus Christ,
        the only Son of God,

eternally begotten of the Father,
God from God, Light from Light,
true God from true God,
begotten, not made,
of one Being with the Father;
through him all things were made.
For us and for our salvation he came down from heaven,
was incarnate from the Holy Spirit and the Virgin Mary,
and was made man.
For our sake he was crucified under Pontius Pilate;
he suffered death and was buried.
On the third day he rose again in accordance with the Scriptures;
he ascended into heaven
and is seated at the right hand of the Father.
He will come again in glory to judge the living and the dead,
and his kingdom will have no end.

We believe in the Holy Spirit, the Lord, the giver of life,
who proceeds from the Father [and the Son]*,
who with the Father and the Son is worshiped and glorified,
who has spoken through the prophets.
We believe in one holy catholic and apostolic Church.
We acknowledge one baptism for the forgiveness of sins.
We look for the resurrection of the dead,
and the life of the world to come. Amen.

---

* The *filioque* [and the Son] is not in the original Greek text. Nevertheless, in the Western Church the *filioque* [and the Son] is customary at worship and is used for the explication of doctrine [*39 Articles of Religion*]. The operative resolution of the College of Bishops concerning use of the *filioque* is printed with the General Instructions at the end of the Holy Communion, Long Form.

The Exhortation and Examination

All are seated except the Ordinands, who stand before the Bishop.

Bishop

It belongs to the Office of a Deacon, to assist the Priest in public worship, especially in the administration of Holy Communion; to lead in public prayer; to read the Gospel, and to instruct both young and old in the Catechism; and at the direction of the Priest, to baptize and to preach. Furthermore, it is the Deacon's Office to work with the laity in searching for the sick, the poor, and the helpless, that they may be relieved.

The Bishop examines the Ordinands as follows

	Will you do this gladly and willingly?
Answer	I will do so, the Lord being my helper.
Bishop	Do you trust that you are inwardly moved by the Holy Spirit to take upon yourself this Office and ministry, to serve God for the promoting of his glory and the edifying of his people?
Answer	I so trust.
Bishop	Do you believe that you are truly called, according to the will of our Lord Jesus Christ, and in accordance with the Canons of this Church, to the ministry of the same?
Answer	I so believe.
Bishop	Are you persuaded that the Holy Scriptures contain all Doctrine required as necessary for eternal salvation through faith in Jesus Christ?
Answer	I am so persuaded.
Bishop	Will you diligently read the same to the people assembled in the church where you are appointed to serve?
Answer	I will.

Bishop	Will you be diligent to frame and fashion your own *lives,* and the *lives* of your *families,* according to the Doctrine of Christ; and to make both *yourselves* and them, as much as in you lies, wholesome examples to the flock of Christ?
Answer	I will do so, the Lord being my helper.
Bishop	Will you reverently obey your Bishop, and other Ministers, who, according to the Canons of the Church, may have charge and authority over you; following with a glad mind and a good will their godly admonitions?
Answer	I will do so, the Lord being my helper.

The congregation shall pray silently for the fulfillment of these purposes.

The Bishop shall pray

Almighty God, our heavenly Father, who has given you a good will to do all these things, grant you also the strength and power to perform the same; that, he accomplishing in you the good work which he has begun, you may be found perfect and without reproach on the last day; through Jesus Christ our Lord. *Amen.*

All may kneel.

The Ordinands shall kneel or lie prostrate, facing the Bishop. The Veni, Creator Spiritus or other hymn to the Holy Spirit may be sung or said as a prayer for the renewal of the Church.

The Ordination of the Deacons

All now stand as witnesses, except the Ordinands, who kneel facing the Bishop.

The Bishop then prays the following prayer, first saying

Let us pray.

O God, most merciful Father, we praise you for sending your Son Jesus Christ, who took on himself the form of a servant, and humbled himself, becoming obedient even to death on a cross. We praise you that you have highly exalted him, and made him Lord of all; and that, through him, we know that whoever would be great must be servant of all. We praise you for the many ministries in your Church, and for calling *these* your *servants* to the Order of Deacons.

Then the Bishop shall lay his hands upon the head of every one to be made Deacon, each one humbly kneeling before him, and he shall say

Receive the Holy Spirit for the Office and Work of a Deacon in the Church of God, now committed to you by the Imposition of Hands; in the Name of the Father, and of the Son, and of the Holy Spirit.

In your great goodness, O Lord, make *this* your *servant* a Deacon in your Church; give *him* grace to be modest, humble, and constant in *his* ministry; give *him* a ready will to observe all spiritual discipline; and with the testimony of a good conscience always before *him*, may *he* continue stable and strong in the service of your Son Jesus Christ, to whom be glory and honor, world without end.

The People in a loud voice respond

AMEN.

The new Deacons may now be vested according to the Order of Deacons.

As the Deacon is vested with a Maniple, the Bishop says

Receive this Maniple as a sign of your service, for your Lord came among us as one who served.

As the Deacon is vested with the Stole, the Bishop says

Receive this Stole as a sign of the yoke of Christ, your Savior.

As the Deacon is vested with the Dalmatic, the Bishop says

Receive this Dalmatic as a sign that you must daily take up the whole armor of God, that you may be able to withstand in the evil day, and having done all, to stand firm.

Then the Bishop shall deliver to every one of them a Book of Gospels or New Testament saying

Take the Authority to read the Gospel in the Church of God and to preach the same.

The Bishop then says to the People

The Peace of the Lord be always with you.

People   And with your spirit.

The liturgy continues with the Offertory. The newly-ordained Deacons prepare the Table.

When the Communion is finished, after the Post-Communion Prayer, the Bishop shall pray the following collect

Go before us, O Lord, in all our doings, with your most gracious favor, and further us with your continual help, that in all our works begun, continued, and ended in you, we may glorify your holy Name, and finally by your mercy obtain everlasting life; through Jesus Christ our Lord. *Amen.*

The Bishop shall then bless the People saying

Our help is in the Name of the Lord;

People   The maker of heaven and earth.

Bishop   Blessed be the Name of the Lord;

People   From this time forth forevermore.

Bishop   The blessing, mercy, and grace of God Almighty,
              the Father, the Son, and the Holy Spirit, be upon you,
              and remain with you forever. *Amen.*

The newly-ordained Deacon dismisses the People saying

Let us go forth into the world rejoicing in the power of the Holy Spirit.

People   Thanks be to God.

From the Easter Vigil through the Day of Pentecost "Alleluia, alleluia" may be added to any of the dismissals.

The People respond

Thanks be to God. Alleluia, Alleluia.

The Form and Manner of Ordaining a Priest

A hymn, psalm, or anthem may be sung.

The People standing, the Bishop says this or an appropriate seasonal greeting

	Blessed be God, the Father, the Son, and the Holy Spirit.
People	And blessed be his kingdom, now and forever. Amen.

In place of the above, from Easter Day through the Day of Pentecost

Bishop	Alleluia. Christ is risen.
People	The Lord is risen indeed. Alleluia.

In place of the above, on Ember days in the season of Lent

Bishop	Bless the Lord who forgives all our sins.
People	His mercy endures forever.

Bishop

Almighty God, to whom all hearts are open, all desires known, and from whom no secrets are hid: Cleanse the thoughts of our hearts by the inspiration of your Holy Spirit, that we may perfectly love you, and worthily magnify your holy Name; through Christ our Lord. *Amen.*

The Presentation

The Bishop and People sit. The Presenters, standing before the Bishop, present the Ordinand, saying

Right Reverend Father in God, we present *N.N.* to be admitted to the Order of Priests.

Bishop	Has *he* been selected in accordance with the Canons of this Church? And do you believe *his* manner of life to be suitable to the exercise of this ministry?

Presenters	We certify to you that *he* has satisfied the requirements of the Canons, and we believe *him* to be qualified for this order.

The Bishop shall then require the Ordinand to take the Oath of Conformity saying

The Canons require that no Deacon may be ordained a Priest in the Church until *he* has subscribed without reservation to the Oath of Conformity. It is also required that each Ordinand subscribe without reservation to the Oath of Canonical Obedience. In the presence of this congregation, I now charge you to make your solemn declaration of these oaths.

The Ordinand then declares

I, *N.N.*, do believe the Holy Scriptures of the Old and New Testaments to be the Word of God and to contain all things necessary to salvation, and I consequently hold myself bound to conform my life and ministry thereto, and therefore I do solemnly engage to conform to the Doctrine, Discipline and Worship of Christ as this Church has received them.

The Ordinand then declares the following Oath of Canonical Obedience as well, saying

And I do swear by Almighty God that I will pay true and canonical obedience in all things lawful and honest to the Bishop of _____, and his successors: So help me God.

The Ordinand then signs the Oath of Conformity and the Oath of Canonical Obedience in the sight of all present.

All stand. The Bishop says to the People

Dear Brothers and Sisters in Christ, you know the importance of this ministry, and the weight of your responsibility in presenting *N.N.* for ordination to the sacred Priesthood. Therefore if any of you know of any impediment or crime because of which we should not proceed, come forward now, and make it known.

If no objection is made, the Bishop continues

	Is it your will that *N.* be ordained a Priest?
People	It is.
Bishop	Will you uphold *him* in this ministry?
People	We will.
Bishop	In peace let us pray to the Lord.

The Litany for Ordinations

All kneel. Then the Bishop or Litanist appointed shall, with the Clergy and People present, say or sing the Litany for Ordinations. The Ordinand shall either kneel or lie prostrate during the Litany.

At the conclusion of the Litany for Ordinations, the Bishop shall stand and pray the following collect, first saying

	The Lord be with you.
People	And with your spirit.
Bishop	Let us pray.

Almighty God, giver of all good things, by your Holy Spirit you have appointed diverse Orders of Ministers in your Church; mercifully behold *this* your *servant* now called to the Office of Priesthood; and so fill *him* with the truth of your Doctrine and adorn *him* with holiness of life, that, both by word and good example, *he* may faithfully serve you in this Office, to the glory of your Name and the edification of your Church; through the merits of our Savior Jesus Christ, your Son, our Lord, who lives and reigns with you and the Holy Spirit, world without end. *Amen.*

The Lessons

Following are the readings appointed for the ordination of a Priest. On a Major Feast, or on a Sunday, the Bishop may select readings from the Proper of the Day.

Isaiah 6:1-8
Psalm 119:33-40
Ephesians 4:7-13 *or* Philippians 4:4-9
Luke 10:1-9 *or* John 10:1-16

The People sit. One or two Lessons, as appointed, are read, the Reader first saying

> A Reading from _____.

A citation giving chapter and verse may be added.

After each Reading, the Reader shall say

> The Word of the Lord.
>
> *People*   Thanks be to God.

Silence may follow. A psalm, hymn, or anthem may follow each Reading.

The Gospel

Then, all standing, the Deacon or other Minister reads the Gospel, first saying

> The Holy Gospel of our Lord Jesus Christ according to
> Saint _____.
>
> *People*   Glory to you, Lord Christ.

After the Gospel, the Reader says

> The Gospel of the Lord.
>
> *People*   Praise to you, Lord Christ.

The Sermon

The Nicene Creed

All stand to recite the Nicene Creed, the Bishop first saying

Let us confess our faith in the words of the Nicene Creed:

Bishop and People

We believe in one God,
    the Father, the Almighty,
    maker of heaven and earth,
    of all that is, visible and invisible.

We believe in one Lord, Jesus Christ,
    the only Son of God,

eternally begotten of the Father,
God from God, Light from Light,
true God from true God,
begotten, not made,
of one Being with the Father;
through him all things were made.
For us and for our salvation he came down from heaven,
was incarnate from the Holy Spirit and the Virgin Mary,
and was made man.
For our sake he was crucified under Pontius Pilate;
he suffered death and was buried.
On the third day he rose again in accordance with the Scriptures;
he ascended into heaven
and is seated at the right hand of the Father.
He will come again in glory to judge the living and the dead,
and his kingdom will have no end.

We believe in the Holy Spirit, the Lord, the giver of life,
who proceeds from the Father [and the Son]*,
who with the Father and the Son is worshiped and glorified,
who has spoken through the prophets.
We believe in one holy catholic and apostolic Church.
We acknowledge one baptism for the forgiveness of sins.
We look for the resurrection of the dead,
and the life of the world to come. Amen.

---

* The *filioque* [and the Son] is not in the original Greek text. Nevertheless, in the Western Church the *filioque* [and the Son] is customary at worship and is used for the explication of doctrine [*39 Articles of Religion*]. The operative resolution of the College of Bishops concerning use of the *filioque* is printed with the General Instructions at the end of the Holy Communion, Long Form.

The Exhortation and Examination

All are seated except the Ordinand, who stands before the Bishop.

The Bishop addresses the Ordinand as follows

You have heard, during the Church's discernment of your vocation and in the Holy Scriptures themselves how weighty is this Office to which you are called. I now exhort you, in the Name of our Lord Jesus Christ, to be a messenger, watchman, and steward of the Lord. You are to teach, to warn, to feed and to provide for the Lord's family; and to seek for Christ's sheep who are in the midst of this fallen world, that they may be saved through Christ forever.

Remember how great is this treasure committed to your charge. They are the sheep of Christ for whom he shed his blood. The Church and Congregation whom you will serve is his bride, his body. If the Church, or any of her members, is hurt or hindered by your negligence, you must know both the gravity of your fault, and the grievous judgment that will result.

Therefore, consider the purpose of your ministry to the children of God. Work diligently, with your whole heart, to bring those in your care into the unity of the faith and of the knowledge of God, and to maturity in Christ, that there be among you neither error in religion nor immorality in life. Finally, equip and lead your congregation to proclaim tirelessly the Gospel of Jesus Christ.

Seeing then that the demands of this holy Office are so great, lay aside all worldly distractions and take care to direct all that you do to this purpose: read, mark, learn and inwardly digest the Scriptures, that you may show yourself both dutiful and thankful to the Lord; and frame your conduct, that of your household, and those committed to your care according to the doctrine and discipline of Christ. Know, however, that you cannot accomplish this of yourself; for the will and the ability needed are given by God alone. Therefore, pray earnestly for his Holy Spirit both to enlighten your mind and strengthen your resolve.

And now, that this congregation of Christ's Church may know your intent in these things, and that your promise may inspire you to your duties; answer plainly these questions, which I, in the Name of God and his Church, now ask you.

Do you believe in your heart, that you are truly called, according to the will of our Lord Jesus Christ, and according to the Canons of this Church, to the Order and ministry of the Priesthood?

Answer   I so believe.

Bishop   Do you believe that the Holy Scriptures contain all doctrine required as necessary for eternal salvation through faith in Jesus Christ? And are you determined, out of the Scriptures to instruct the people committed to your charge; and to teach nothing as necessary to eternal salvation but that which may be concluded and proved by the Scriptures?

Answer   I believe it, and have so determined, by God's grace.

Bishop   Will you then give your faithful diligence always so to minister the doctrine, sacraments, and discipline of Christ, as the Lord has commanded and as this Church has received them, according to the Commandments of God, so that you may teach the people committed to your charge with all diligence to keep and observe them?

Answer   I will, by the help of the Lord.

Bishop   Will you be ready, with all faithful diligence, to banish and drive away from the Body of Christ all erroneous and strange doctrines contrary to God's Word; and to use both public and private admonitions and exhortations, to the weak as well as the strong within your charge, as need shall require and occasion shall be given?

Answer   I will, the Lord being my helper.

Bishop   Will you be diligent in prayer, and in the reading of Holy Scripture, and in such study as may further the knowledge of the same, laying aside the study of the world and the flesh?

Answer   I will, the Lord being my helper.

Bishop   Will you be diligent to frame and fashion your own life, and that of your family, according to the doctrine of Christ; and to make both yourself and them, as much as you are able, wholesome examples and patterns to the flock of Christ?

Answer   I will, the Lord being my helper.

Bishop   Will you maintain and set forward, as much as you are able, quietness, peace, and love among all Christian people, and especially among those who are or shall be committed to your charge?

Answer   I will, the Lord being my helper.

Bishop   Will you reverently obey your Bishop, and other chief Ministers, who, according to the Canons of the Church, may have charge and authority over you, following with a glad mind and will their godly admonitions, and submitting yourself to their godly judgments?

Answer   I will, the Lord being my helper.

The congregation shall pray silently for the fulfillment of these purposes.

The Bishop shall pray

Almighty God, our heavenly Father, who has given you a good will to do all these things, grant you also the strength and power to perform the same; that, he accomplishing in you the good work which he has begun, you may be found perfect and without reproach on the last day; through Jesus Christ our Lord. *Amen.*

All may kneel. The Ordinand shall kneel or lie prostrate, facing the Bishop. The Veni, Creator Spiritus shall be sung or said as a prayer for the renewal of the Church.

Veni, Creator Spiritus

Come, Holy Ghost, our souls inspire,
And lighten with celestial fire.
Thou the anointing Spirit art,
Who dost Thy sevenfold gifts impart.

Thy blessed unction from above,
Is comfort, life, and fire of love.
Enable with perpetual light
The dullness of our blinded sight.

Anoint and cheer our soiled face
With the abundance of Thy grace.
Keep far our foes, give peace at home;
Where Thou art guide, no ill can come.

Teach us to know the Father, Son,
And Thee, of both, to be but One;
That, through the ages all along,
This may be our endless song

Praise to Thy eternal merit,
Father, Son, and Holy Spirit.

The Consecration of the Priest

All now stand as witnesses, except the Ordinand, who kneels facing the Bishop.

The Bishop then prays the following prayer, first saying

Let us pray.

Almighty God, and heavenly Father, who, in your infinite love and
goodness towards us, has given to us your only and most dearly
beloved Son Jesus Christ, to be our Redeemer, and the Author of
everlasting life; who, after he had made perfect our redemption by his
death, and was ascended into heaven, sent into the whole world his
Apostles, Prophets, Evangelists, Pastors, and Teachers; by whose
labor and ministry he gathered together a great flock in all parts of

the world, to set forth the eternal praise of your holy Name: For these great benefits of your eternal goodness, and because you have called *this* your *servant* here present to the same Office and ministry, appointed for the salvation of all people, we offer to you our most hearty thanks; we praise and worship you; and we humbly ask you, through your blessed Son, that we and all who call upon your holy Name, may continue to show ourselves thankful to you for these and all your other benefits; and that we may daily increase and go forward in the knowledge and faith of you and your Son, by the Holy Spirit. So that as well by *this Minister*, as by those entrusted to *his* care, your holy Name may be forever glorified, and your blessed kingdom enlarged.

The Bishop with the Priests present shall lay their hands upon the head of each one to receive the Order of Priesthood; the Ordinand humbly kneeling, and the Bishop saying

Receive the Holy Spirit for the Office and Work of a Priest in the Church of God, now committed to you by the Imposition of our Hands. If you forgive the sins of anyone, they are forgiven. If you withhold forgiveness from anyone, it is withheld. Be a faithful minister of God's holy Word and Sacraments; in the Name of the Father, and of the Son, and of the Holy Spirit.

The Bishop shall then pray the following over the Ordinand.

Send your heavenly blessing upon *this* your *servant*; that *he* may be clothed with righteousness, and that your Word, spoken by *his* mouth, may have such success, that it may never be spoken in vain. Grant also, that we may have grace to hear and receive what *he* shall deliver out of your most holy Word as the means of our salvation; that in all our words and deeds we may seek your glory, and the increase of your kingdom; through Jesus Christ our Lord, who lives and reigns with you in the unity of the Holy Spirit, world without end.

The People in a loud voice respond

AMEN.

The new Priest may now be vested according to the Order of Priests.

As the Priest is vested with a Stole, the Bishop says

Take the yoke of the Lord, for his yoke is easy and his burden is light.

As the Priest is vested with the Chasuble, the Bishop says

Receive this priestly garment which symbolizes charity; for God is well able to give you an increase of charity and a perfect work.

The Bishop then anoints the hands of the new Priest, saying

Grant, O Lord, to consecrate and sanctify these hands by this unction, and by our blessing; that whatsoever they bless may be blessed, and whatsoever they consecrate may be consecrated and sanctified; in the Name of our Lord Jesus Christ. Amen.

The Bishop then gives the new Priest a Bible in one hand and a Chalice in the other hand saying

Take authority to preach the Word of God and to administer the Holy Sacraments. Do not forget the trust committed to you as a Priest in the Church of God.

The Bishop then says to the People

	The Peace of the Lord be always with you.
People	And with your spirit.

The liturgy continues with the Offertory. Deacons prepare the Table.

Standing at the Holy Table, with the Bishop and other Ministers, the newly-ordained Priest joins in the celebration of the Holy Communion and in the Breaking of the Bread.

When the Communion is finished, after the Post-Communion Prayer, the new Priest shall pray the following collect

Go before us, O Lord, in all our doings, with your most gracious favor, and further us with your continual help, that in all our works begun, continued, and ended in you, we may glorify your holy Name, and finally by your mercy obtain everlasting life; through Jesus Christ our Lord. *Amen.*

The Bishop shall then bless the People saying

Our help is in the Name of the Lord;
People The maker of heaven and earth.
Bishop Blessed be the Name of the Lord;
People From this time forth forevermore.
Bishop The blessing, mercy, and grace of God Almighty,
the Father, the Son, and the Holy Spirit, be upon you,
and remain with you forever. *Amen.*

Or, at his direction, the Bishop may ask the newly-ordained Priest to bless the People saying

The peace of God which passes all understanding keep your hearts
and minds in the knowledge and love of God, and of his Son Jesus
Christ our Lord; and the blessing of God Almighty, the Father, the
Son, and the Holy Spirit, be among you, and remain with you always.
Amen.

The Deacon dismisses the People saying

Let us go forth into the world rejoicing in the power of
the Holy Spirit.
People Thanks be to God.

*From the Easter Vigil through the Day of Pentecost "Alleluia, alleluia" may be added to
any of the dismissals.*

The People respond

Thanks be to God. Alleluia, Alleluia.

The Form and Manner of Ordaining and Consecrating a Bishop

The Archbishop normally presides at the Consecration of a Bishop; however, the Archbishop may choose to designate another bishop to be the Chief Consecrator. When this happens, all rubrics referring to the Archbishop shall be taken to mean "Chief Consecrator."

A hymn, psalm, or anthem may be sung.

The People standing, the Archbishop says this or an appropriate seasonal greeting

Blessed be God, the Father, the Son, and the Holy Spirit.
People And blessed be his kingdom, now and forever. Amen.

In place of the above, from Easter Day through the Day of Pentecost

Archbishop Alleluia. Christ is risen.
People The Lord is risen indeed. Alleluia.

In place of the above, on Ember days in the season of Lent

Archbishop Bless the Lord who forgives all our sins.
People His mercy endures forever.

Archbishop

Almighty God, to whom all hearts are open, all desires known, and from whom no secrets are hid: Cleanse the thoughts of our hearts by the inspiration of your Holy Spirit, that we may perfectly love you and worthily magnify your holy Name; through Christ our Lord. *Amen.*

The Presentation

The Archbishop and People sit.

The Bishop Elect, properly vested, shall be presented to the Archbishop by at least two Bishops of this Church, the Bishops who present him saying

Most Reverend Father in God, we present to you N.N., a godly and well-learned man, to be Ordained and Consecrated Bishop.

Then shall the Archbishop require Testimonials from the Secretary of the College of Bishops and the President of the Standing Committee regarding the person presented for Consecration, and shall cause them to be read.

The Archbishop shall then require the Bishop Elect to take the Oath of Conformity saying

The Canons of this Church require that no Priest may be consecrated as a Bishop in the Church until he has subscribed without reservation to the Oath of Conformity. In the presence of this congregation, I now charge you to make your solemn declaration of the same.

The Bishop Elect then declares

I, *N.N.*, do believe the Holy Scriptures of the Old and New Testaments to be the Word of God and to contain all things necessary to salvation, and I consequently hold myself bound to conform my life and ministry thereto, and therefore I do solemnly engage to conform to the Doctrine, Discipline and Worship of Christ as this Church has received them.

The Bishop Elect then declares the following Oath of Canonical Obedience as well, saying

And I do swear by Almighty God that I will pay true and canonical obedience in all things lawful and honest to the Archbishop of this Church, and to his successors: So help me God.

The Bishop Elect then signs the above Oath of Conformity and Oath of Canonical Obedience in the sight of all present.

Then the Archbishop invites the congregation present to pray, saying

Dear Brothers and Sisters in Christ, it is written in the Gospel of Saint Luke that our Savior Christ continued the whole night in prayer, before he chose and sent forth his twelve Apostles. It is written also in the Acts of the Apostles, that the disciples at Antioch fasted and prayed before they sent forth Paul and Barnabas by laying their hands upon them. Let us, therefore, following the example of our Savior and his Apostles, offer up our prayers to Almighty God, before we admit and send forth this person presented to us, to do the work to which we trust the Holy Spirit has called him.

The Litany for Ordinations

All kneel. Then the Archbishop or Litanist appointed shall, with the Clergy and People present, say or sing the Litany for Ordinations. The Bishop Elect shall either kneel or lie prostrate during the Litany.

At the conclusion of the Litany for Ordinations, the Archbishop shall stand and pray the following collect, first saying

	The Lord be with you.
People	And with your spirit.
Archbishop	Let us pray.

Almighty God, who by your Son Jesus Christ gave many excellent gifts to your holy Apostles, and charged them to feed your flock; give your grace to all Bishops, the Pastors of your Church, that they may diligently preach your Word, duly administer your Sacraments, and wisely provide godly Discipline; and grant to your people that they may obediently follow them, so that all may receive the crown of everlasting glory, through the merits of our Savior, Jesus Christ, your Son, our Lord, who lives and reigns with you and the Holy Spirit, world without end. *Amen.*

The Lessons

Following are the readings appointed for the ordination of a Bishop. On a Major Feast, or on a Sunday, the Archbishop may select readings from the Proper of the Day.

Isaiah 61:1-11
Psalm 100
1 Timothy 3:1-7 *or* Acts 20:17-35
John 21:15-19 *or* John 20:19-23 *or* Matthew 28:18-20

The People sit. One or two Lessons, as appointed, are read, the Reader first saying

A Reading from _____.

A citation giving chapter and verse may be added.

The Word of the Lord.

People   Thanks be to God.

Silence may follow. A psalm, hymn, or anthem may follow each Reading.

The Gospel

Then, all standing, the Deacon or other Minister reads the Gospel, first saying

The Holy Gospel of our Lord Jesus Christ according to
Saint _____.

People   Glory to you, Lord Christ.

After the Gospel, the Reader says

The Gospel of the Lord.

People   Praise to you, Lord Christ.

The Sermon

The Nicene Creed

All stand to recite the Nicene Creed, the Archbishop first saying

Let us confess our faith in the words of the Nicene Creed:

Archbishop and People

We believe in one God,
    the Father, the Almighty,
    maker of heaven and earth,
    of all that is, visible and invisible.

We believe in one Lord, Jesus Christ,
    the only Son of God,
    eternally begotten of the Father,
    God from God, Light from Light,
    true God from true God,
    begotten, not made,

of one Being with the Father;
through him all things were made.
For us and for our salvation he came down from heaven,
was incarnate from the Holy Spirit and the Virgin Mary,
and was made man.
For our sake he was crucified under Pontius Pilate;
he suffered death and was buried.
On the third day he rose again in accordance with the Scriptures;
he ascended into heaven
and is seated at the right hand of the Father.
He will come again in glory to judge the living and the dead,
and his kingdom will have no end.

We believe in the Holy Spirit, the Lord, the giver of life,
who proceeds from the Father [and the Son]*,
who with the Father and the Son is worshiped and glorified,
who has spoken through the prophets.
We believe in one holy catholic and apostolic Church.
We acknowledge one baptism for the forgiveness of sins.
We look for the resurrection of the dead,
and the life of the world to come. Amen.

The Exhortation and Examination

All are seated except the Bishop Elect, who stands before the Archbishop.

The Archbishop addresses and examines the Bishop Elect as follows

Brother, the Holy Scriptures and the ancient Canons command that
we should not be hasty in laying on hands, and admitting any person
to authority in the Church of Christ, which our Lord purchased with
no less price than the shedding of his own blood; so before we admit

---

* The *filioque* [and the Son] is not in the original Greek text. Nevertheless, in the
Western Church the *filioque* [and the Son] is customary at worship and is used for
the explication of doctrine [*39 Articles of Religion*]. The operative resolution of the
College of Bishops concerning use of the *filioque* is printed with the General
Instructions at the end of the Holy Communion, Long Form.

you to this Office, we will examine you in certain Articles, in order that this congregation here present may know how you will conduct yourself in the Church of God.

Are you persuaded that you are truly called to this ministry, according to the will of our Lord Jesus Christ, and the Order of this Church?

Answer   I am so persuaded.

The following questions are addressed to the Bishop Elect by one or more of the bishops.

Question   Are you persuaded that the Holy Scriptures contain all Doctrine required as necessary to eternal salvation through faith in Jesus Christ? And are you determined out of the Holy Scriptures to instruct the people committed to your charge; and to teach or maintain nothing as necessary to eternal salvation, but that which you shall be persuaded may be concluded and proved by the same?

Answer   I am so persuaded, and determined, by God's grace.

Question   Will you then faithfully study the Holy Scriptures, and call upon God by prayer for the true understanding of them; so that you may be able by them to teach and exhort with wholesome Doctrine, and to withstand and convince those who contradict it?

Answer   I will do so by the help of God.

Question   Are you ready, with all faithful diligence, to banish and drive away from the Church all erroneous and strange Doctrine contrary to God's Word; and both privately and publicly to call upon others and encourage them to do the same?

Answer   I am ready, the Lord being my helper.

Question   Will you renounce all ungodliness and worldly lusts, and live a godly, righteous, and sober life in this present world; that you may show yourself in all things an

	example of good works for others, that the adversary may be ashamed, having nothing to say against you?
Answer	I will do so, the Lord being my helper.
Question	Will you maintain and set forward, as much as shall lie in you, quietness, love, and peace among all people, and diligently exercise such discipline as is, by the authority of God's Word and by the Order of this Church, committed to you?
Answer	I will do so, by the help of God.
Question	Will you be faithful in examining, ordaining, sending, and laying hands upon others?
Answer	I will, by the help of God.
Question	Will you show yourself gentle, and be merciful for the sake of Christ, to poor and needy people and to all those in need of help?
Answer	I will with God's help.

The congregation shall pray silently for the fulfillment of these purposes.

The Archbishop shall pray

Almighty God, our heavenly Father, who has given you a good will to do all these things, grant you also the strength and power to perform the same; that, he accomplishing in you the good work which he has begun, you may be found perfect and without reproach on the last day; through Jesus Christ our Lord. *Amen.*

All may kneel.

The Bishop Elect shall kneel or lie prostrate, facing the Archbishop. The Veni, Creator Spiritus shall be sung or said over him as follows

Veni, Creator Spiritus

Come, Holy Ghost, our souls inspire,
And lighten with celestial fire.
Thou the anointing Spirit art,
Who dost Thy sevenfold gifts impart.

Thy blessed unction from above,
Is comfort, life, and fire of love.
Enable with perpetual light
The dullness of our blinded sight.

Anoint and cheer our soiled face
With the abundance of Thy grace.
Keep far our foes, give peace at home;
Where Thou art guide, no ill can come.

Teach us to know the Father, Son,
And Thee, of both, to be but One;
That, through the ages all along,
This may be our endless song:

Praise to Thy eternal merit,
Father, Son, and Holy Spirit.

The Consecration of the Bishop

All now stand as witnesses, except the Bishop Elect, who kneels facing the Archbishop.

The Archbishop prays the following Prayer of Consecration, first praying

	Lord, hear our prayer;
People	And let our cry come to you.

Archbishop

Almighty God, and most merciful Father, of your infinite goodness you have given your only Son Jesus Christ to be our Redeemer, and to be the author of everlasting life. After he had made perfect our redemption by his death and resurrection, and was ascended into heaven, he poured down his gifts abundantly upon his people, making some Apostles, some Prophets, some Evangelists, some Pastors and Teachers, for edifying and perfecting his Church. Grant to this your servant such grace, that he may be ever ready to propagate your Gospel, the good news of our reconciliation with you; and use the authority given to him, not for destruction, but for salvation; not for hurt, but for help; so that, as a wise and faithful steward, he will give to your family their portion in due season, and so may at last be received into everlasting joy.

Then the Archbishop, and at least two other Bishops, shall lay their hands upon the head of the Bishop Elect, the Archbishop and other Bishops saying

Receive the Holy Spirit for the Office and Work of a Bishop in the Church of God, now committed to you by the Imposition of our Hands; in the Name of the Father, and of the Son, and of the Holy Spirit.

The Archbishop then continues

Most merciful Father, send down upon this your servant your heavenly blessing; so endue him with your Holy Spirit, that he, in preaching your holy Word, may not only be earnest to reprove, beseech, and rebuke, with all patience and Doctrine; but may he also, to such as believe, present a wholesome example in word, in conversation, in love, in faith, in chastity, and in purity; that, faithfully fulfilling his course, at the Last Day he may receive the crown of righteousness, laid up by the Lord Jesus, our righteous Judge, who lives and reigns with you and the same Holy Spirit, one God, world without end.

The People in a loud voice respond

AMEN.

The new Bishop is now vested according to the Order of Bishops. During the presentations that follow, the Archbishop may be assisted by others.

The Archbishop shall present the new Bishop with the Holy Scriptures, saying

Give heed to reading, exhorting, and teaching. Think upon the things contained in this Book. Be diligent in them, that your growth in the grace and knowledge of our Lord Jesus Christ may be evident to all; in doing this you shall save both yourself and those who hear you. Be to the flock of Christ a shepherd, not a wolf; feed them, do not devour them; hold up the weak, heal the sick, bind up the broken, bring back the lapsed, seek the lost. Do not confuse mercy with indifference; so minister discipline, that you forget not mercy; that when the Chief Shepherd appears, you may receive the never fading crown of glory; through Jesus Christ our Lord. *Amen.*

The Archbishop presents him with a Pastoral Staff saying

Take this Staff and watch over the flock of Christ.

The Archbishop may anoint the forehead of the new Bishop with the Oil of Chrism saying

Receive the anointing of this oil, and remember continually to stir up the grace of God which is given to you; for God has not given us the spirit of fear, but of power, and love, and self control.

The Archbishop may give him a Pectoral Cross saying

Receive this Cross; remember that he whom you serve reconciled us by his own blood.

The Archbishop may give him an Episcopal Ring saying

Take this Ring; be faithful to the Bride of Christ.

The Archbishop may give him the Miter saying

Receive this Miter, and remember that the authority rests in God's Word and Holy Spirit.

The Archbishop then says to the People

        The Peace of the Lord be always with you.

People   And with your spirit.

Standing at the Holy Table, with the Archbishop and other Ministers, the newly consecrated Bishop joins in the celebration of the Holy Communion and in the Breaking of the Bread.

When the Communion is finished, after the post-communion prayer, the new Bishop shall pray the following collect

Go before us, O Lord, in all our doings, with your most gracious favor, and further us with your continual help, that in all our works begun, continued, and ended in you, we may glorify your holy Name, and finally by your mercy obtain everlasting life; through Jesus Christ our Lord. *Amen.*

The Archbishop, or at his direction the newly-consecrated Bishop, shall then bless the People saying

	Our help is in the Name of the Lord;
People	The maker of heaven and earth.
Bishop	Blessed be the Name of the Lord;
People	From this time forth forevermore.
Bishop	The blessing, mercy, and grace of God Almighty, the Father, the Son, and the Holy Spirit, be upon you, and remain with you forever. *Amen.*

The Deacon dismisses the People saying

	Let us go forth into the world rejoicing in the power of the Holy Spirit.
People	Thanks be to God.

From the Easter Vigil through the Day of Pentecost "Alleluia, alleluia" may be added to any of the dismissals. The People respond

Thanks be to God. Alleluia, Alleluia.

The Litany and Suffrages
for Ordinations

Other petitions may be added with the consent of the Ordinary.

O God the Father,
Have mercy on us.

O God the Son,
Have mercy on us.

O God the Holy Spirit
Have mercy on us.

O holy Trinity, one God,
Have mercy on us.

We beseech you to hear us good Lord; and that it may please you to
grant peace to the whole world, and to your Church;
We beseech you to hear us, good Lord.

That it may please you to sanctify and bless your holy Church
throughout the world;
We beseech you to hear us, good Lord.

That it may please you to inspire all Bishops, Priests, and Deacons
with the love of you and your truth.
We beseech you to hear us, good Lord.

That it may please you to endue all Ministers of your Church with
devotion to your glory and to the salvation of souls;
We beseech you to hear us, good Lord.

Here at the Ordination of Deacons and of Priests shall be said

That it may please you to bless *these* your *servants*, now to be admitted
to the Order of Deacons (*or* Priests), and to pour your grace upon
them; that *they* may duly execute *their* Office to the edification of your
Church, and to the glory of your holy Name;

We beseech you to hear us, good Lord.

Here at the Consecration of a Bishop shall be said

That it may please you to bless this our Brother selected, and to send your grace upon him, that he may duly execute the Office to which he is called, to the edification of your Church, and to the honor, praise, and glory of your Name;
We beseech you to hear us, good Lord.

That it may please you to guide by your indwelling Spirit those whom you call to the ministry of your Church; that they may go forward with courage, and persevere to the end;
We beseech you to hear us, good Lord.

That it may please you to increase the number of Ministers in your Church, that the Gospel may be preached to all people;
We beseech you to hear us, good Lord.

That it may please you to grant us true repentance, amendment of life and the forgiveness of all our sins;
We beseech you to hear us, good Lord.

That it may please you to hasten the fulfillment of your purpose, that your Church may be one;
We beseech you to hear us, good Lord.

That it may please you to grant that we, with all your saints, may be partakers of your everlasting Kingdom;
We beseech you to hear us, good Lord.

Lord, have mercy
Christ, have mercy.
Lord, have mercy.

Hear us, O Lord, when we cry out to you;
Have mercy upon us and hear us.

O Lord, arise and help us;
And deliver us for your Name's sake.

Let your priests be clothed with righteousness;
And let your saints sing with joy.

Lord, hear our prayer;
And let our cry come to you.

General Information
on this
Edition of the Ordinal

- Liturgies within this Ordinal are authorized for use without alterations to the text as given herein. Alterations to the Eucharistic liturgy may be made only if permitted within that rite.

- The language and Doctrine of this edition of the Ordinal is descended from the historic Anglican Ordinals of 1549, 1662, and the American 1928 and Canadian 1962. The primary source for this document was the American book of 1928 because it has removed references to the English Monarch and Government, which makes more sense in our North American context. The other editions are used in places where there has been a variance between the various editions. Additionally, Peter Toon's *An Anglican Prayer Book*, Preservation Press, 2008, was frequently consulted.

- The structure of this edition, however, does look to ecumenical and more recent Anglican Ordinals, especially the American BCP of 1979, the Church of England *Common Worship: Ordination Services*, Study Edition of 2007, and the Province of Southern Africa *An Anglican Prayer Book* of 1989. The Ordo for all three Orders has been given a common outline to make the Liturgies more parallel to one another, thus making them easier to follow.

- The *Veni, Creator Spiritus* remains in traditional language for its poetic qualities as an ancient hymn of the Church.

- Where appropriate, this edition seeks to reconcile the text of the Ordinal with the English Standard Version of the Bible.

- Since the historic Anglican Ordinals did not provide for an Old Testament reading or a Psalm, this edition consulted both the American BCP of 1979 and the Church of England, *Common Worship: Ordination Services*, Study Edition of 2007. The Epistle and Gospel readings are those found in the historic Ordinals.

- This edition restores a more accurate translation of "et cum spiritu tuo" as "and with your spirit." For more information, please see Peter Toon's explanation of the phrase in, *An Anglican Prayerbook*, Preservation Press, 2008, pg. 44.

- When the word "Minister" is used in this document, it refers to someone in one of the three Holy Orders: Bishops, Priests, or Deacons.
- In some places, a black line along the left side of the page indicates that the material in that section may be used at the discretion of the Bishop or Archbishop presiding at that Liturgy.
- It is suggested that future drafts of this Ordinal include forms for the Consecration of a Church, for the Institution of Ministers, and for the Installation of an Archbishop.
- The ordination Liturgy may be re-cast from contemporary (you, your, yours) to traditional (thee, thine, they) idiom when desired.
- Throughout the entire ordinal, language referring to the number of ordinands (he/them) has been placed in italics. This is to aid the presider in shifting plural language to singular, and singular to plural. This is also the case when referring to the gender of the ordinand (in the liturgies for the ordination of Deacons and Priests).
- Rubric texts should be retained and should be altered only as necessary.
- A Maniple may be bestowed at the vesting of a Priest or a Bishop as it is at the vesting of a Deacon.